MINI-14

Super
Systems

MINI-14

Super Systems

DUNCAN LONG

PALADIN PRESS
BOULDER, COLORADO

Other books by Duncan Long:

AK47: The Complete Kalashnikov Family of Assault Rifles
AR-7 Super Systems
The AR-15/M16: A Practical Guide
AR-15/M16 Super Systems
Automatics: Fast Firepower, Tactical Superiority
Combat Ammunition: Everything You Need to Know
Combat Revolvers: The Best (and Worst) Modern Wheelguns
Combat Rifles of the 21st Century: Futuristic Firearms for
   Tomorrow's Battlefields
The Mini 14: The Plinker, Hunter, Assault, and Everything Else Rifle
Modern Ballistic Armor: Clothing, Bomb Blankets, Shields, Vehicle
   Protection . . . Everything You Need to Know
Modern Sniper Rifles
Powerhouse Pistols: The Colt 1911 and Browning Hi-Power
   Sourcebook
The Ruger .22 Automatic Pistol: Standard/Mark I/Mark II Series
Streetsweepers: The Complete Book of Combat Shotguns
The Sturm, Ruger 10/22 Rifle and .44 Magnum Carbine
The Terrifying Three: Uzi, Ingram, and Intratec Weapons Families

Mini-14 Super Systems
by Duncan Long
Copyright © 1991 by Duncan Long

ISBN 0-87364-589-8
Printed in the United States of America

Published by Paladin Press, a division of
Paladin Enterprises, Inc., P.O. Box 1307,
Boulder, Colorado 80306, USA.
(303) 443-7250

Direct inquires and/or orders to the above address.

CONTENTS

ACKNOWLEDGMENTS

T hanks must go to the manufacturers who so graciously loaned accessories for inspection and testing for the writing of this book, and especially to Linda M. DeProfio of Sturm, Ruger & Company, Inc., for her above-and-beyond-the-call-of-duty help.

As has been the case with my other books, a number of companies, including Federal Cartridge Company, Olin/Winchester, Omark, Action Arms, and PMC, helped to keep me supplied with several types of ammunition for testing the firearms and modifications outlined in this publication.

Thanks must go to Peder Lund, Jon Ford, and the other fine people at Paladin Press for producing this book. A thank you should also go to my dad for his work in processing several of the photos in the book, as well as to the many experimenters, gunsmiths, manufacturers, and hobbyists who have given me ideas and suggestions on ways to—and ways not to—customize the Mini-14 rifle.

And, of course, the usual very special thanks to Maggie, Kristen, and Nicholas for their continued patience and help.

INTRODUCTION

The Mini-14 is an inexpensive and dependable rifle for which a wealth of aftermarket accessories is available. This makes it easy to turn it into your own "super-system" firearm that ideally suits your needs.

As most readers probably know, the Mini-14 was designed by Bill Ruger, who launched his designing career with the marketing of a successful .22 auto pistol in 1949 and an improved Western-style revolver that took advantage of the fast-draw craze of the 1950s.

Despite its name, the Mini-14 is not just a scaled-down M14 rifle, though it certainly has that appearance. In fact, it's an outgrowth of the Garand and M-14 .30-caliber rifles, with some notable improvements. The gas port has been moved back so it's inside the stock, and parts of the receiver and trigger group have been refined and strengthened.

The Mini-14 carries a relatively low price tag because many of its parts are made using a process known as "investment casting." This process was pioneered by Ruger, and it creates super-strong parts with a minimum of machining. The modern industrial machinery and the simple design and layout of Ruger's firearms, coupled with investment casting of many parts, has allowed Sturm, Ruger & Company to produce high-quality firearms that are relatively inexpensive.

When it was introduced in 1972, Ruger's Mini-14 was aimed at the law-enforcement and military markets. Because demand was great in the U.S. civilian market, the company offered a "sporterized" semiauto version with a 5-round magazine in 1976.

Strangely enough, while no large military sales were ever secured, the rifle sold like crazy in the civilian market as well as to small police departments who were often strapped for money. The rifle quickly became a great commercial success, and Ruger was so swamped with orders that it built a new complex devoted entirely to manufacturing Mini-14s.

In addition to its low price (which is often only half that of most military-style rifles on the market), the Mini-14 boasts a traditional look, with its wooden stock and blued metal. This is in sharp contrast to most .223 rifles, which are modeled after military weapons. Those who abhor the plastic furniture and parkerized metal of assault rifles find the down-home, hunting-rifle look of the Mini-14 very pleasing. (And since plastic stocks in a variety of styles are also available as aftermarket accessories, those who want a "military look" have that option as well with the Mini-14. Best of all, the cost of a Mini-14 and a second military-style stock is still considerably less than that of other .223 semiauto rifles.)

Sturm, Ruger & Company has improved the Mini-14's design over the years. In early Mini-14s, certain parts had a tendency to wear out with extended use, but in the newer guns these parts have been strengthened and modified. Additional models have also been added to the Ruger Mini-14 lineup, giving the buyer an even greater choice in terms of variations of the firearm.

There are several series of the Mini-14. Early-production 180 Series Mini-14s (denoted by the "180" in the serial number) have a slightly different overall design and different specifications than later models; many accessories won't fit on these guns. The 181 and later series are the "improved" versions and are more desirable as far as durability is concerned. The post-1988 guns have a 1-in-7 barrel twist (rather than 1-in-10), which is more ideal both for combat and hunting.

There are three distinct models of the Mini-14: a semiauto sporting version with a military-style rear sight (the Mini-14/5); a police/military-style rifle, often with bayonet lug and flash suppressor (classified as the Mini-14/20GB or, with selective fire, as the AC-556); and a Ranch Rifle (M-14/5R), which has an integral scope mount molded into the receiver and a flip-down rear peep sight that accommodate scope use.

Within these three major model

The Ranch Rifle version of the Mini-14 has a small, tilt-down rear sight. Note the straighter butt on the stock. Like newer models of the standard Mini-14, the Ranch Rifle has a handguard that keeps the hand off the operating lever. (Photo courtesy of Sturm, Ruger & Company.)

groupings, there is a wide range of options, including stainless-steel parts (denoted by a "K" prefix on the model number), folding stocks ("F" prefix), 5-round magazines ("5" suffix), 20-round magazines ("20" suffix), 30-round magazines ("30" suffix), flash suppressor/grenade launcher/bayonet lug ("GB" suffix). The Ranch Rifle is offered in a choice of .223 or 7.62x39mm chamberings (the latter is marketed as the Mini-30).

The configurations of the Mini-14 that are available to the public all reflect legal restrictions and political pressures from gun-grabbing groups. The folding stock, bayonet lugs, selective fire, and magazine capacity all have been restricted at one time or another by Sturm, Ruger & Company as well as by legislators in various states. For much the same reason, alternate chamberings for the Mini-14 are found on the European market, where the ownership of guns capable of firing military rounds is restricted. The most common of these is the .222 Remington, which is nearly identical to the .223 Remington in performance. (For a more complete look at variations of the Mini-14 and its history, see my book *The Mini-14: The Plinker, Hunter, Assault, and Everything Else Rifle*, available from Paladin Press.)

For the Mini-14 owner, the wide range of variations available serves as the basis for a super system. In addition, the excellent basic design of the rifle doesn't dictate the need for a stock behind the receiver, meaning the hobbyist can easily create bullpups, folding stocks, or even pistol versions of the gun. The barrel of the Mini-14 can easily be chopped without ruining the functioning of the weapon. This would be impractical with most other semiauto rifles (though legal considerations will enter in here as well, as we'll see later).

Adding to the customizing potential of the Mini-14 are aftermarket plastic stocks, flash hiders, scope mounts, and so forth. These make it possible for the do-it-yourselfer to reshape and alter the basic layout of the rifle extensively, achieving a factory-finished look with a minimum of effort.

With all these facts in mind, I've written this book to serve as a guide for those wishing to have a rifle that fits their body, needs, and pocketbook. For the more advanced hobbyist, I've also tried to outline the information and techniques needed to create a truly one-of-a-kind Mini-14 rifle that will not only generate a lot of double takes but also deliver—whether at the shooting range, in the field when hunting, or during critical moments of self-defense.

In short, this book will show you how to create, with a little work and thought, a rifle unlike any other that is perfect for your needs: a Mini-14 super system.

CHAPTER 1

Tools for the Amateur Gunsmith

Most of the basic Mini-14 modifications in this book can be done with a few simple hand tools that are commonly available. Even the more extensive modifications can be done—though not quite as neatly or quickly—with common tools. Almost none of the tasks outlined in this book call for expensive milling machines, metal lathes, or even drill presses. Instead, most require only know-how, the willingness to invest some elbow grease, and the patience to take your time to do things right.

Doing things right can't be emphasized too much. A do-it-yourself project that's sloppy will produce a malfunctioning firearm that's dangerous and often doesn't give you a second chance. You could end up trashing your Mini-14, perhaps causing an injury or even a death in the process. Never rush when you're working on your Mini-14. It's also essential to understand when to leave things alone. Tackling work you're uncomfortable with is unwise and unsafe. If any of the operations outlined in this book seem unclear to you or you feel they're too difficult for your skills, don't hesitate to have a gunsmith make the modifications for you. It's always better to spend a few dollars with a gunsmith than to wind up with a dangerous firearm.

Amateur gunsmithing encompasses a lot of different tasks. It can be as simple as smoothing a sharp edge on a piece of plastic or metal or as complex as rebarreling a Mini-14. Some "amateur" work actually falls in the territory of professional tasks (and is therefore far beyond the scope of this book). If the amateur gunsmithing projects delineated in this book intrigue you, you may wish to pursue more complex ventures that are actually professional work. You can do this by enrolling in a quality school that teaches gunsmithing (see Appendix C).

Much useful information can also be gleaned from other books, including The National Rifle Association's (NRA's) *Gunsmithing Guide—Updated*, J.B.Wood's *Gunsmithing: The Tricks of the Trade*, Robert A. Steindler's *Home Gunsmithing Digest*, and others (see Appendix B). Two books containing the secrets and tricks of some six hundred gunsmiths are Brownells' *Gunsmith Kinks*, Vol. I and II. These will give the amateur a wealth of insight into the various ways of carrying out modifications and repairs of firearms. Brownells' *The Machinist's Bedside Reader* is another excellent book that gives numerous insights into gunsmithing and making parts for firearms, as well as detailing how to make specialized gunsmithing tools with shop equipment.

Regardless of the level of work you're engaged in, there are three rules that must be stressed. First, be sure your Mini-14 is unloaded before you attempt to do any modifications; second, wear protective goggles when doing any gunsmithing work; and third, protect your fingers and skin from the various tools you'll be using, which can cut, gouge, and smash your digits and other precious bits of anatomy. Obey these rules and exercise some common sense and your projects will remain safe.

That said, let's look at a few of the basic tools you will be using. Chances are good you already have most of them; you may wish to purchase others as required.

Anvil

You don't need a blacksmith's four-hundred-pound anvil to work on a Mini-14. But sometimes it's necessary to have a hard surface for hammering, peening, or reshaping a part. Then an anvil is essential. Your anvil need not cost much. It can simply be a large piece of scrap steel liberated from a local junk pile or scrap-metal yard. Cutoff ends of I-beams, short lengths of railroad track, or what have you will work perfectly well. The main thing is to get a chunk of steel with enough weight to hold it down and a flat surface that will allow work to be placed on it. Some bench vises also have small anvils built into one end. These work for small jobs, but don't try to use it for massive reshaping or you'll undoubtedly wreck your vise in the process.

Calipers

When it comes to duplicating parts or creating new pieces, a good caliper is an essential tool to own. A direct-reading caliper with a built-in scale is a must for taking precise readings. It's just too easy to make errors with the slide-rule-type caliper, which requires careful reading and figuring to obtain the actual measurement (though it can be useful for directly transferring and comparing sizes between parts).

Metal calipers last much longer than plastic ones, but they're also more expensive. If you have much work to do, get quality metal calipers from B-Square or Brownells (see Appendix A). If you'll only be using calipers once in a while, purchasing a plastic set like those offered by RCBS makes good sense.

Center Punch

Whether you're drilling holes in metal, plastic, or wood, a center punch is essential for getting the hole started in the right place. The center punch is positioned where the center of the hole to be drilled should be and then tapped with a small mallet. This leaves a small indentation on the surface and keeps the drill bit from wandering during the operation.

Punches allow you to test the hardness of metal before attempting to drill it; if the punch can't easily mark the metal, it's a safe bet that the drill won't work well either. Discovering this with the punch is less traumatic than trying to drill into the metal and breaking or dulling the bit and scarring up the metal surface in the process.

Clamps

Clamps can be used to hold parts together when gluing, welding/soldering/brazing, or shaping pieces. As such, they are often more useful than another pair of hands. C-clamps are the most versatile, though other types may be handy for some jobs. If you need to purchase clamps for a project, buy several sizes so you'll be able to accommodate a variety of projects in the future.

Dremel Tool

The Dremel tool can be very useful to the amateur gunsmith. Like most other power tools, though, it can also get you into trouble really quickly, so you need to exercise a little bit of judgment when using it.

A small motor powers the Dremel tool. Small bits and grinding wheels can be placed into its chuck to tackle a variety of chores. Almost anything a Dremel tool can do, a file, drill, grinder, or stones can do, though not as fast. Therefore, you can get along without a Dremel tool, but chances are that once you have one you'll be glad you bought it and will discover you use it all the time. If you plan to do a lot of gunsmithing work, consider purchasing a Dremel tool. You can probably locate one from a local hardware store or from a company like Brownells.

Drift Punch

The drift punch is used to push out small pins holding various parts of the trigger group and other areas of the Mini-14 together. It's not essential to buy punches, since you can actually make your own with just a little file work on an old nail or other scrap metal. Quality punches can be found at Brownells, B-Square, or most hardware stores.

Drill Press

The drill press is one of the most useful tools you can have when it comes to making parts or accessories for a Mini-14. However, you can achieve nearly the same ends with a power drill by strapping the hand tool to a table or into a vise. Even so, the drill press can do the work more precisely and will exhibit less wobble in its bit (and this can be important if you're working on really small parts).

When you're drilling a hole in metal, plastic, or wood with a drill press or power drill, there are tricks that will make the task easier. Most important is to use a center punch to mark the hole's center. This will ensure that the hole is aligned properly under the drill bit and help keep the bit from wandering when the hole is being started.

Cutting oil is essential when drilling steel and is of help with aluminum or brass, but it isn't necessary for drilling plastic, wood, or other soft materials. It is available at most hardware stores that sell drill bits. To use cutting oil, simply put a drop into the groove of a drill bit and another on the point where you'll be drilling. Replace the oil as the drilling progresses. If the friction of the bit creates smoke, reduce the pressure on the bit and add more oil.

Use only sharp bits when drilling holes. Old bits can be resharpened and used for some time. There are special tools that will allow you to sharpen bits with a small grinding wheel. It's also possible to use a whetstone to sharpen the bits (and this is considerably cheaper than purchasing a special tool). If you do use a whetstone, be sure to maintain the original angles of the bit's blade.

Take care to run the drill at the correct speed when cutting through metal or other materials. Consult your owner's manual for recommended speeds. Generally, the harder the material, the slower the bit should move.

You'll discover that tempered metals aren't easy to drill. The route to take with these is to anneal them—softening the metal by heating it and then allowing it to cool slowly. After annealing and working the metal, you must reharden or temper it by heating it and then cooling it quickly (usually by immersing it in water or oil).

Both annealing and tempering are tricky. The metal can generally be annealed with a propane torch until it turns the proper color (the color varies with the type of steel). Once this color is achieved, the flame is moved away very slowly so that the temperature drops very slowly. To temper the metal, the piece is reheated and then quenched in oil or water after the proper color has again been reached. When the exact hardness isn't critical, most amateur gunsmiths can do a fairly good job at tempering metal. But when things get critical—as with a trigger or hammer—then the job is better left to the experts. For those really interested in learning how to do this work, it is wise to study a book like Brownells' *Gunsmith Kinks, Vols. I and II* carefully and experiment first with scrap steel.

Some metal parts only have hardened surfaces. It is therefore sometimes possible to drill these parts by using a stone or Dremel tool to cut a nick through the surface and then use a drill to cut into the softer metal that has been exposed.

Once a hole is drilled, its sharp edges will usually have to be removed. This process, known as "chamfering," can be done with a drill bit larger than the one used to drill the original hole. You hold the bit in your hand and turn it in the hole to remove the sharp edge. This can also be done with a drill, but the bit can get jammed in the smaller hole if you aren't careful.

A drill press can also be used for types of lathe work to shape small, short parts. To do this, a metal rod is fastened into the drill chuck and a file or hacksaw blade cuts the metal as it spins. Care should be taken to keep the file or saw blade moving so the teeth don't heat up and melt. Hardened steel parts can be "turned" if a stone or Dremel tool with a grindstone is used to cut the metal.

A hacksaw blade can be used to make narrow cuts in metal pieces in the spinning chuck. If you wish to have a number of grooves evenly spaced, mount two hacksaw blades together with a spacer between them. If one blade is upside down, its toothless edge will be placed in the groove that has already been cut to hold the other blade in its proper spacing and alignment as it cuts the next groove.

A hacksaw blade can also be used to cut a piece to length when the work in a drill chuck is nearly finished; just be careful the part doesn't fly off and become lost—or hit you in the face.

When you're doing this "poor-man's lathe work," stop the drill from time to time to check the metal part you're working on. If size is critical, use your calipers regularly. Don't run the drill for extended periods of time when doing lathe work or you'll risk overheating the motor. Lathe work done on a drill press can be very precise. In fact, it can rival that of a lathe costing thousands of dollars if you take the time to do it right.

A table vise can be a very useful gadget for your drill press. A table vise allows objects fastened to the press to move along two planes and permits simple milling-type operations to be performed on the press. If you add a table vise to your drill press, you'll need a longer post to accommodate it. Therefore, large, milling-type vises are best used with floor presses. A useful accessory for the table vise is a jig designed to hold round stock in the clamp; this can be used with standard vises as well, making it practical to own.

Prices of table vises vary greatly; if you buy one with plastic rotary parts, you can generally save some money without sacrificing too much in terms of performance. Brookstone carries such vises at reasonable prices.

Router bits, milling bits, metal bits, and wood bits can all be employed with varying results when using a drill press on wood or plastic. These special bits make it possible to do a wide range of cutting and milling with nearly as good a result as with a router (though the cut won't be quite as smooth due to the drill's lower speed).

Files

Files have been called the "poor-man's milling machine." Little wonder—Third-World gunsmiths create whole firearms from scrap metal, using only files and a few other hand tools.

You'll discover that you can't have too many files if you do a lot of gunsmithing work. But it's wise to start with a small assortment of files until you discover which are the most useful. Once you have a good idea of what you need, buy more.

Flat, triangular, and round (chain saw) files are all very useful for various types of shaping tasks. Small "Swiss" or "needle" files are helpful for hard-to-reach areas or for finishing tiny parts. Most of the files you'll probably need can be purchased at your local hardware store, but you may also want to try Brownells, Brookstone, or B-Square for some extra-special files. (B-Square offers excellent sets of fine-cut and medium-cut needle files for $20 a set.)

Be sure to protect your files. If they rub against each other on your bench or in a tool box, they will become dull quickly. Use new files to work on hard metal and steel, then relegate them to cutting softer metals or plastic as their teeth become dull.

Most files come without handles. You can actually work with them this way, but you'll discover that handles make them easier to use. Fortunately, wooden handles can be purchased for very little and can be reused after a file wears out. To mount a wooden handle on a file, slowly drive the tang of the file into the hole in the handle. Some companies also market a detachable/interchangeable handle for files. These are okay, but you'll likely discover that they're more work than they're worth as you change back and forth.

Some gunsmiths create an expedient handle for files by simply wrapping rags around the tang. This creates a soft handle that's comfortable to work with, though wrapping each tang as you use it gets to be somewhat of a hassle.

The file should be lifted on its return stroke when cutting. This allows shavings to drop out of the teeth so the next cut can be made more efficiently and so cleaning the file won't be such a chore. Avoid getting oil in a file; oil will trap particles in the teeth. Do use a wire brush to clean files from time to time. This is especially important when cutting aluminum since it can build up on the file and actually start scratching deep grooves into the metal being shaped.

To create a rounded finish on smooth surfaces, rock the file while pushing it across the surface. To cut flat surfaces, keep the file perfectly parallel to the work. A concave surface along one plane can be created with a round file.

You don't have to do all file work by holding the tang end of the file. Often you can make cuts at the right angle of the normal path of the file (so it moves across the work sideways). When doing this, you can use both hands to hold each end of the file. This allows you to apply a lot of pressure to your work and causes less fatigue to your fingers.

Occasionally, you'll discover you need to work on a corner of a piece, removing metal from one surface but not from another. In such a case, a good trick is to grind off one or more faces of your file so they can't cut into the metal. This makes it possible to use one side of the file to cut, while only its smooth face rubs against a part of the metal that is not to be cut. The same end can be achieved by using masking tape on various areas of a metal piece where it's not to be cut or by attaching tape to the file's surface.

Coarse-toothed files are good for starting a project because they remove maximum amounts of material. As your work comes closer to completion, finer-toothed files will offer better control and keep the finish on the work smoother. Fine files that have worn teeth can be used to polish the surface of the work when you're rounding things up.

Grinder

Grinding wheels can be very effective for shaping or altering metal parts and may be essential for working hardened parts. Grinding wheels can create excessive heat through friction; therefore, it's wise to have a small container of water into which you can dip a part being ground from time to time. Some people also hold small parts in their fingers when working on a grinder; this allows them to feel if they're overheating the part, but it's also a little dangerous since it's easy to grind your fingers against the wheel.

The cost of grinders varies. Usually, you can pick up a fairly good one at a discount store. An alternative is a do-it-yourself grinder. This type of grinder uses an old electric motor with a large shaft that has an adapter (available at most hardware stores) that allows you to mount a grinding wheel on the electric motor. Provided you already have the motor, you can create a grinder for around $15 by going this route. All you need to add is a metal strap to anchor the motor in place.

Hacksaws

Hacksaws can do a wide variety of gunsmithing jobs, from shortening barrels to cutting small, hardened metal parts. In addition to making thin cuts, hacksaws can be used to sharpen file cuts or even do milling-type jobs by mounting blades alongside each other to make wide cuts.

Sawtooth counts vary on hacksaw blades. As with files, you'll often discover that the initial work is best done with coarser teeth, while fine teeth (with a lower tooth count) are best suited for final work or when a smooth finish is desired.

Hacksaws can also be used as a sort of thin file. As such, the hacksaw is useful in creating screw slots or accomplishing similar projects. This technique is especially useful in changing the many accessories that are slotted for hex wrenches so they can be tightened with a standard screwdriver, which is more apt to be available when you're in the field and the part comes loose. To make this conversion, simply cut a slot into the hex-head bolt with the hacksaw blade. If you're careful, you can also leave the bolt head so it can still be used with a hex wrench as well.

If you wish to modify an accessory so it doesn't require a screwdriver to tighten it, you can cut a slot into a hex-head bolt and then silver-solder a coin or other small bit of metal into the slot to create a wing bolt. This makes it simple to tighten the accessory in the field, and thus should be considered essential for equipment that might be used for self-defense.

Hammers

Regular clawed hammers can be employed in some gunsmithing tasks. Much more useful are rubber mallets, tack hammers, and ball peen hammers. Plastic- and brass-faced hammers can also be essential. B-Square offers an excellent brass hammer. Think before you use a hammer. This tool can quickly trash a piece with peening marks or bend it into the wrong shape.

Ice Cube Trays and Egg Cartons

Perhaps the most unlikely gunsmithing tools are old ice cube trays and egg cartons, but they are ideal for holding small parts. If you don't use something to hold them, the pieces will sooner or later roll off your workbench onto the floor. You'll likely never see the part again—or you'll waste an inordinate amount of time on your hands and knees searching for it. (Much gunsmithing work seems to take place in the form of searching for parts on the floor of the shop. When you discover yourself doing this despite your best efforts to avoid it, place a high-intensity light on the floor. This will often cause the small part to cast a long shadow, making it more readily apparent to your searching eye. *Never* work over carpet!)

Junk Bins

While junk bins aren't technically tools, they can be as useful to you as anything else you own when it comes to fabricating parts and customizing your Mini-14. Good junk bins should be divided by the size and type of materials stored in them. Steel, plastic, and wood scraps can all be utilized in creating and modifying accessories for the Mini-14. Rods, bolts, and screws can all prove to be invaluable from time to time and may even spark an idea. When in doubt, do not throw it out. Instead, dismantle scrap materials and add them to your junk bin.

Junk bins don't need to take up a lot of room or appear sloppy. In fact, your junk bins should be arranged carefully to allow you to inspect what you have and quickly locate pieces by size. Therefore, the dimensions of bins should vary from small boxes for tiny parts, screws, and bolts, to large closets for containing lengths of wood or large metal parts.

Lathe

A metal lathe can be very useful in "turning" tubular-shaped parts. Larger metal lathes can even be utilized to contour, rechamber barrels, or do similar work. However, much amateur lathe work can be done using the techniques outlined above for the drill press. Therefore, unless you're interested in tackling really complex metal-working jobs, you're better off saving your money for other, more essential tools.

If you decide to purchase a metal lathe, don't be tempted to go with a mini-lathe unless you only want to create small parts. The mini-lathes have motors that are underpowered for many jobs, and their size is a major limitation. A 6-inch lathe will probably be the smallest you should consider, and a 10-inch one is better.

Micrometer

Some advanced amateur gunsmiths may wish to purchase a micrometer, but it's been my experience that calipers can do almost anything a micrometer can—plus a whole lot more, like taking inside diameter measurements of holes and, with their tail, finding the depths of dead-end holes as well. If in doubt, purchase good metal calipers rather than a micrometer.

Milling Machine

If you're really serious about doing gunsmithing work, it would be nice if you had one of these. With a milling machine, you can create or duplicate almost any metal part, including the receiver or bolt of a Mini-14. But the high cost of this machine is prohibitive unless you're going to be using it extensively.

Fortunately, most milling work can be done on a drill press or with a file and hacksaw. The work is slower and requires greater care to achieve precision, but the tradeoff in monetary savings makes the extra effort worthwhile for most amateur gunsmiths. So unless you want to become a full-time gunsmith or machinist, save your money and buy other tools.

Pliers

Pliers are among the more useful tools for most gun-smithing work, and you'll need a variety of them for some tasks. Needle-nose pliers and standard pliers will accommodate most work on the Mini-14. Occasionally, vise-grip pliers can be useful. (Vise-grip pliers can double as a small vise when you're working on tiny parts; you may even wish to fasten them onto your bench vise to hold a part while you work on it.) Regular or needle-nose pliers can also be transformed into mini-vise-grips by wrapping rubber bands around their handles after a piece is positioned in their jaws.

Power Drill

The drill press is more useful than a power drill for working on firearms, but many home shops have a power drill instead of a drill press. If this is the case in your shop, you may wish to forego the expense of a drill press and make do with the power drill you already own.

The 3/8-inch capacity chuck accommodates more jobs than a 1/4-inch chuck. A drill with variable speed adapts to a variety of materials, with slower speeds being ideal for steel and harder stock while higher speeds are best reserved for working with wood. Reverse switches or "hammer" modes aren't of value for most gunsmithing jobs.

Occasionally, you'll see a drill stand that accommodates a power drill in order to transform it into a drill press. Such makeshift arrangements are generally less than satisfactory since most drills have shafts that wobble around. This makes precise work impossible, especially on small parts. Additionally, getting the drill in and out of the press is time-consuming, so you practically have to dedicate it to serving as a drill press. You might—as one amateur gunsmith once did—end up buying a second drill to use as a power drill so the other can remain as a press! My advice: if you need a drill press, spend a little extra and buy a "low-end" drill press rather than a power-drill stand.

The guidelines for drill bits used in a drill press should be applied to power-drill bits as well: always use a punch to start holes, utilize cutting oil when drilling in steel, and keep the bits sharp.

Propane Torch

A small propane torch that runs off miniature bottled gas containers can be purchased at local hardware stores. These propane torches can be adapted to a variety of chores, from soldering to brazing to heat tempering. For advanced do-it-yourselfers, it's even possible to cast small parts from brass, aluminum, or plastic by melting the material and pouring it into molds. The molds can be created from plaster of paris (molded from wax or other models) or carved into soft stone or plaster. Such work is practical, provided the cast parts are small.

Regardless of how you use your propane torch, be sure to have adequate ventilation in your work area. Dangerous fumes are often produced by the torch as well as the materials being heated.

Router

Since the Mini-14 has a wooden stock, a router can sometimes be of use when working on it. If you wish to create a second wooden stock for your rifle (to experiment with a different stock configuration or as the basis of a bullpup, perhaps), then a duplicator can be a useful accessory to a router.

With a duplicator, you can use your original stock as the pattern to construct a second stock quickly from lumber. Once the inside of the second stock has been modified so it will fit your Mini-14, you're free to shape its exterior contours to suit your particular tastes and needs. (It should be noted that plastic can be shaped as well as wood with a router, though you should do a little experimenting before tackling any major jobs.)

Take care to keep router blades sharp and your fingers clear of the spinning blade. Next to the power saw, this is one of the most dangerous tools in a shop. Be cautious, don't daydream, and use goggles when working with a router.

This is another tool you'll seldom need, but if you already have a router in your shop it can be useful in fabricating stocks.

Screwdrivers

The Mini-14 has two large screws on either side of its stock. These have to be removed when taking the stock reinforcement insert and forearm liner out of an old stock to put them into an aftermarket stock. While a standard screwdriver will work, a gunsmithing screwdriver with a very narrow blade is best. These special screwdrivers are less apt to "bugger up" the screw slot than the standard screwdriver with its wedge-shaped blade.

Purchasing a gunsmithing screwdriver for this one small task is not cost-effective. Instead, select a standard screwdriver that matches the side screws of your Mini-14 and modify its blade. This can be done by carefully filing off the side of the screwdriver blade so it has scooped rather than wedge-shaped sides.

If you find yourself working with a number of different guns from time to time, then buying a set of gunsmithing screwdrivers does make sense. The Chapman Screwdriver Set is ideal. It contains twelve slotted blades and two Phillips-head screwdriver bits that fit into a screwdriver handle or the handle extension that comes with the kit, along with a convenient carrying case and rachet assembly. The Chapman Screwdriver Set is available from Brigade Quartermasters for $23. (Note: all prices were current when this book went to press; changes may have occurred since.)

Screw-Pitch Gauge

This tool isn't essential, but it can be handy if you're doing a lot of do-it-yourself work on the Mini-14. The pitch gauge consists of a thin piece of metal with teeth that match up to the threads on a screw or bolt. Once you've matched the correct gauge to the screw or bolt, you know the number of threads per inch (known as the screw's "pitch").

B-Square offers a handy set of these gauges mounted like blades in a pocketknife so they're all in order and impossible to lose (there is a metric set as well as one that uses U.S. measurements). Get the American-standard gauges for working with the Mini-14 and most of its U.S.-made accessories.

While this tool isn't essential for do-it-yourself work, it can quickly pay for itself by allowing you to purchase the correct screws or bolts at a local hardware store or through a mail-order source (or even discover them in your junk bins *without* having to try each one out to see if it has the proper threads). At $11.95, B-Square's set is considerably less expensive than buying replacements from a manufacturer.

Soldering Iron

An electric soldering iron sounds like an unlikely tool for gunsmithing work, but many of the new nylon-based plastics used in stocks and accessories can be joined by positioning them together and then heating up their edges until they melt and run together. The plastic solidifies when it cools off and the two parts are then joined. This selective melting can be done easily with an electric soldering iron. Visit your local Radio Shack or other hobbyist store and get a small soldering "pencil"; don't be tempted to purchase a soldering gun—it's too expensive, and it's awkward to work with for many jobs.

You'll have to experiment with your soldering iron to learn how much melting to do in order to join parts. You'll also find that you can use plastic scraps to build up areas, reshape stocks, and take care of other odds and ends when doing custom work on a Mini-14. Plastic in your junk bin can be an important asset when working with modern firearms accessories. Do be careful with the fumes from the solder or plastic. These can be a veritable witches' brew of carcinogens and acidic gases, so adequate ventilation from a fan is essential. Also, be sure to use the correct solder. Acid-core solder is designed for use in joining metal parts. Resin core is for electrical soldering. Don't get the two mixed up or your job will be considerably more difficult. Finally, don't try to join large metal parts with the soldering iron. It doesn't generate enough heat. Instead, use a propane torch.

Spray Paint

Spray paint makes it possible, with a little care, to place a durable, professional-looking finish on both the Mini-14 and its accessories quickly. Your local discount store will have a wide array of colors and paints to choose from which, for just a few dollars, will allow you to quickly change your Mini-14 from a fluorescent orange hunting rifle to a camouflaged military-style gun.

The secret to obtaining good spray-painted finishes is to first clean the metal, plastic, or wood with some type of degreaser so the paint will adhere. Outers Crud Cutter is ideal for this purpose; acetone (fingernail polish remover) will work, too.

Another important technique in applying spray paint is to go slowly and evenly to prevent the paint from running. Slowly build up the finish while allowing a little time for the paint to dry. The extra time taken with a can of spray paint will determine whether you end up with a smooth, even finish or one marred by runs and drips.

Those wanting a firearm that won't reflect light should choose flat paint. Gloss, or even semigloss, will create a reflective finish that is not ideal for hunting or self-defense. If you'll be painting your Mini-14's barrel, use paint designed for automotive engine blocks, which is heat-resistant. (Avoid barbecue grill paint. While it's heat-resistant, it tends to rub off.)

"Designer Black" seems to be the most common color used on today's firearms. But by no means should you limit yourself to this shade. Combinations of green, black, and brown can be used to create very good camouflage patterns; use masking tape or even just leaves and branches piled over your Mini-14 between the different colors being applied.

Spray-painting the metal parts on a Mini-14 is probably most effective on the stainless-steel models since rust is less likely to develop under the paint. Whether you're painting blued or stainless-steel guns, do take extreme care to keep the paint from interfering with the operation of the firearm. This means you should avoid getting paint inside the receiver or barrel, on the bolt, or in the trigger group. A very light coat of paint is always better than a heavy one that interferes with the operation of the firearm.

Epoxy paint gives the most durable finish you can spray onto a firearm. It's also a headache to apply smoothly and get it to set up properly. Often, results are less than desirable and, unlike enamel paint that can be removed with acetone, epoxy paint tends to stay in place forever. Therefore, you'd be wise to use enamel spray paint and avoid epoxy unless you're *very certain* of what you're doing.

Also, take pains to avoid getting epoxy paint on your skin or breathing its fumes since many people have serious allergic reactions to it. (Once it's dry, it's no longer dangerous, however.) Never spray any kind of paint unless you have adequate ventilation. When possible, wear a good paint mask, do your spraying outside, and stay upwind of the spray particles.

Taps and Dies

A tap is a small tool that allows you to cut threads into a hole you've drilled in metal or plastic. As such, it can be very useful when you need to join parts or mount accessories on a firearm.

Taps generally come in sets. One of the taps from such a set, the taper tap, is designed to start the threading of a hole. The plug tap is used to finish the task. If you have a dead-end or "blind" hole (which is very hard to thread and is best avoided when possible), then you'll also use a bottoming tap.

Hardware stores usually have taps, but only in the more common threadings, which are *not* used in most gunsmithing work. Therefore, while these taps may be of use for other do-it-yourself projects, they won't be suitable if you're using gun accessories with screws of greater-than-normal pitch. For such projects, you'll need to purchase taps and wrenches from Brownells or B-Square.

As with drilling holes into metal, tapping requires cutting oil; failure to use oil will cause damage to a tap. In order to succeed, you'll also need to work slowly—don't hurry unless you enjoy seeing things break.

The hole drilled to be tapped must be slightly larger than the minor diameter of the screw and smaller than the outer diameter of the screw. There are formulas to determine which bit to use for which screw, but in practice, it's often easier to measure the screw's smallest and largest diameter and choose a bit accordingly.

Once you've drilled the hole, use a tap wrench to hold the tap and start the taper tap into the hole. When using this tap, be sure to apply a liberal amount of cutting oil to its threads and the hole. Be conscientious in positioning the tap so it's perpendicular to the hole. That accomplished, apply a little downward pressure to the taper tap as you turn it clockwise a half turn.

When using the taper tap (as well as the other two taps), you need to back off a quarter turn for each half or full turn. This breaks off the small chip of metal cut by the tap. Failure to do this will clog up the cut and ruin the tap.

Once the taper tap is started, you can quit applying downward pressure; the threads will pull the tap down. No downward pressure is exerted with the other two taps. Use only your clockwise torque to cut the threads once you've got them started.

If one of the three taps sticks, work it gently back and forth. *Never* try to force a tap free since its tempered metal will snap apart. Treat taps as though they're brittle—because they are.

When you're cutting a blind hole (one that doesn't go clear through the metal), you should stop from time to time and clear the chips from the hole as well as from the bottoming tap. If possible, drill blind holes slightly deeper than the length of the screw that will go into them to give yourself a little extra leeway in cutting the threads.

Always keep the piece being tapped securely fastened with a vise. This will help to keep the threads square and prevent the tap from breaking.

If you have a drill press, B-Square's Tru-Tapper ($39.95) can really simplify your work and is a must if you'll be threading many screw or bolt holes. It can also double as your tap holder. Drill the hole into the metal part using your drill press, then leave the part positioned on the drill table and replace the drill bit with the Tru-Tapper. It is then turned by hand while riding perfectly perpendicular to the hole, held in place by the press' chuck.

Don't buy a whole set of taps unless you're sure you'll be using them. It's much better to purchase just a few quality taps that you really need and save your money.

A die makes it possible to cut threads on metal rods to create bolts or screws. This, too, can enable you to create a wide range of accessories and fasten them in place on your Mini-14. Just don't get sidetracked making screws by hand that are readily available from other sources—it's expensive and time-consuming.

When cutting threads with a die, be sure to fasten the rod being cut into a vise, use cutting oil, and go slowly. Grinding a slight chamfer onto the end of the piece being threaded so it will fit into the die more easily is always a good idea. Apply a little pressure to get the die started while turning the diestock (the tool that holds the die).

The diestock should be turned back frequently to break the chips created in the new thread. Back off a quarter turn for each half or full turn. Once the thread is started, you can quit applying downward pressure on the stock since the threads will pull the die downward.

Thread the stock only as far as is actually needed. When you're finished, check the thread to be sure it's square and isn't too tight a fit. If it is too tight, you need to readjust the die and go over the threads again to cut away the extra metal.

Tin Snips

Tin snips are scissorlike devices that are good for cutting all types of light sheet metal as well as rubber, leather, or thin plastic. These tools aren't essential, but they can certainly be useful for a variety of cutting tasks.

Utility Knives

Utility knives can be used for all kinds of cutting and shaping of wood or plastic. The thin blade quickly slices through materials that thicker blades can barely cut. Buy an inexpensive utility knife at a hardware store and keep its blade sharp with a whetstone.

Vise

A vise is ideal for holding parts that are being drilled or filed. And it's essential for much of the precision work you'll be doing. Unlike some of the other tools, you can't skimp when buying a vise. Cheap vises wear out quickly and aren't very secure from the start.

It isn't essential to have a vise with a swivel base or an anvil face at its rear. These features (or the lack thereof) shouldn't determine whether or not you purchase a given model. If you mount a vise properly, you'll seldom need the swivel feature. Pounding on—and possibly damaging—a quality vise rather than working on an anvil is not the wisest of actions!

When working on soft objects, you can use leather, rubber, cardboard, or lead plates to protect parts from being scarred by the steel jaws. Mount your vise where it's easy to get at but not in the way when you're not using it. Mounting a nonrotating vise on the corner of the workbench allows you to use it from two sides. A corner mount also leaves the rest of the bench clear so you can work without running into the vise.

Welding Machine

Welding is a quick way to join pieces of metal by melting them together so they become one piece (often with the addition of metal from a welding rod). This makes building complex accessories for the Mini-14—or even attaching them to it—a snap. A weld, properly done, is very strong; it is the ideal way to join parts that will be seeing a lot of man-handling.

A welding rig is a big-ticket item; don't buy one for an occasional job. In some cities you may be able to rent a rig, but generally it's easier to take the piece to a machine shop and have them do the work for you. However, if you're interested in being able to repair metal furniture and tools, fabricate tools and accessories, or complete similar tasks, then a welder may be just the thing you need.

There are two common types of welding rigs: gas and electric. Gas requires bottles that have to be refilled and wrestled around. Also, the process of welding with gas warps the metal slightly, so you have to take that into account or end up with a deformed product.

Arc welders use household current and don't warp the metal. For this reason, they're generally better suited for small do-it-yourself projects. If you end up with either type, remember that welding is an art, and practice and training are called for before you'll acquire any skill at it. Welding can also be dangerous, so be sure to observe all precautions and wear protective goggles and clothing.

Whetstones

Whetstones are used to sharpen tools. They're also excellent for working on hardened metal parts like those in a Mini-14's trigger group. (Of course, work on hardened parts should always be approached with great care since such parts often have critical dimensions. Altering the shape of such a part can lead to firearm malfunctions and possibly a dangerous situation.)

The more the merrier when it comes to whetstones. Get coarse as well as smooth stones and curved as well as squared shapes. Your local hardware store will be a good source.

Wire Cutters

Wire cutters are useful for shortening springs and screws. They're also excellent "nibblers" that can be used to cut out small portions of plastic on accessories that need to be altered. Nibbling is also faster than filing and is therefore good for coarse shaping of plastic or aluminum parts when you're building accessories for the Mini-14.

Wood Chisels

These tools are necessary for work on plastic or the stock of a Mini-14. Keep the chisel blades sharp and use a wooden or rubber mallet (rather than brute strength) to help propel the chisel through whatever you're cutting.

Most nylon-based plastics cut like wood, only without the grain. When cutting wood or plastic with the chisel, first outline the area to be removed; when you start removing material, this cut will keep you from accidentally running into the area that is intended to remain behind. When chiseling out material, work toward the outline cut you've already made. After you've removed most of the material from an area, carefully smooth it with a wide-bladed chisel. This will give your work a smooth, professional-looking finish.

Wood Rasps

Wood rasps are very useful for shaping both wood and plastic. Rasps should be handled like files: don't let them rub together, don't let their teeth get clogged, and use a variety of rasps according to the job at hand.

Work with coarse-toothed rasps first and save the finer ones for finishing work to minimize sanding. (You may also discover that metal files will save some sanding work in the finishing of wood or plastic.)

Wood Saws

Coping saws, band saws, and other woodworking saws can be very useful from time to time in cutting plastic and wooden stocks or other Mini-14 accessories.

Coping saws, with the proper blades, will even tackle aluminum or mild steel. Don't get the cheapest coping saw you can find; it should be capable of being adjusted so that cuts can be made with the blade at any angle. Get a good supply of blades and this tool will do a surprising number of fine cutting chores.

Another useful tool is the carpenter's saw. Provided it has fine teeth, it can be used to shorten stocks or make other smooth cuts. Fine teeth will take longer to cut but will generally require less cleanup.

To make really smooth cuts when altering stocks or other parts that must be cut precisely, use masking tape to delineate the area to be cut as well as to protect the area that will remain behind.

Workbench

This may not seem like a real tool, but in fact, a good bench is one of the more important things you need to do quality do-it-yourself work on the Mini-14. If you're just doing a little work, you can get by with a desk or kitchen table. Otherwise, chances are you'll damage the work surface or be unable to do the work properly.

A workbench allows you to use a vise or even nail your work to the bench's surface to keep it in place. You can't do that with a kitchen table (not if you wish to keep your spouse from shooting you, at least).

Heavier benches are preferable to lighter ones since they stay in place when you're hammering. The surface of the workbench should be strong enough to support a heavy load. Carpeting one section of the bench or putting a soft cloth or plastic foam pad over it will allow you to place a

Mini-14 on the bench's surface without having to worry about scratches.

Wrenches

An adjustable crescent wrench can be of use with many accessories for the Mini-14. However, fixed crescent wrenches are considerably better than adjustable ones if you can afford a set.

There are many other tools that can be utilized in working on and modifying a Mini-14. Regardless of the tools you're using, be sure to take your time and do your best work so you can be proud of it when you're done. Don't launch into projects without giving some thought to what you're doing, and be sure the job is worth doing and that you're capable of handling it.

CHAPTER 2

Customizing Your Mini-14

L ike anything that's mass-produced, the Mini-14 (and its sister rifle, the Mini-30) has to be compromised a bit to accommodate everyone: short and tall, shooters and hunters, policemen and civilians, and so forth. But it's simple to change the rifle to a considerable degree in order to make it suit *your* build. This will go far toward improving your shooting as well as the enjoyment you get out of using the rifle.

As with most other rifles, the most glaring Mini-14/Mini-30 mismatch for tall, thin shooters—as well as for short or muscular users—is in the length of pull (the distance between the trigger and the butt of the rifle). The ideal length of pull places the buttplate of a rifle a tad short of the inside of the shooter's elbow (when bent at 90 degrees) when his finger is on the trigger. (It should be noted that those shooting from prone positions or from rifle rests sometimes prefer a slightly longer length of pull than is dictated by their size. Such shooters may therefore wish to increase the length of pull slightly more than is indicated by the above standard.)

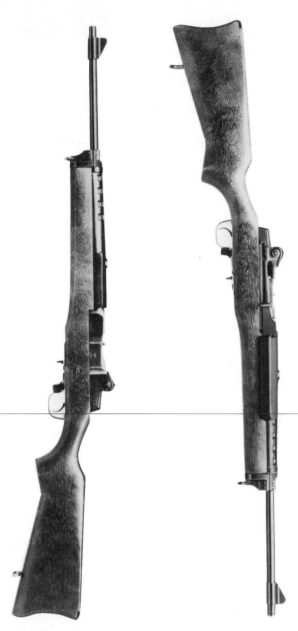

The standard Mini-14 stock has a shape that many find comfortable, but the overall pull will be short for some shooters. (Photo courtesy of Sturm, Ruger & Company.)

Length of pull is important to a shooter. Too short a length of pull and your arm gets cramped; too long a pull and there's a bit of a problem when shouldering the Mini-14. Adding to your woe is the fact that the length of pull you need changes with the seasons. Wearing a thin T-shirt will call for a longer pull, while your winter coat dictates a shorter pull.

There are several easy ways to change the Mini-14's length of pull. For those using the rifle in areas where there are wide temperature swings, a slip-on buttpad makes it possible to change the length of pull quickly by simply removing or adding the pad.

E&L Manufacturing makes an excellent $10 slip-on buttpad for the Mini-14 (the small size fits both the standard Mini-14 and Mini-30 stocks). The black rubber pad comes with an insert that allows the pad itself to be adjusted for an even longer or shorter pull for still more flexibility.

For a more permanent reduction of the length of pull, it's possible to cut off the stock and remount the plastic factory buttplate or add a new recoil pad. Generally, this is a job for a gunsmith. But skilled amateurs may wish to tackle the task and will be able to do a good job, provided they go slowly and carefully.

The more difficult route is to remount the factory plate after cutting the stock. If you elect to do this, you must follow the curve of the original stock carefully and then chisel the butt so it can accommodate the plate that normally covers it. It's a lot of tedious effort.

A better way to reduce the overall length—or add to it—is to cut the stock off square and then add a conventional rubber recoil pad to the butt. Before you start cutting at a stock, it's wise to do some careful figuring—any wood you remove is hard to put back on.

Remember that the recoil pad will add to the length of pull. Therefore, you need to determine the length of pull you need (the distance from where your finger comfortably meets the trigger to the crook of your elbow) and then measure it on your Mini-14 stock. To determine the amount you need to cut from the butt of the stock, you then subtract the thickness of the recoil pad you'll be adding to the stock and *add* the thickness of your saw cut (saw into a bit of scrap wood and then measure the width of the cut).

Once you know how much you need to cut, your next step is to measure carefully. Then wrap a piece of fiberglass packing tape around the stock, with the edge of the tape at the point where the cut will be made and the bulk of the tape protecting the portion of the stock that will remain with the Mini-14.

After visibly checking the tape to be sure it's square, use a fine-tooth carpenter's saw to do the cutting. Take time to be sure everything is correct before starting your saw cut. The extra time in measuring and checking pays off in a job well done.

After the cut is made, leave the tape in place to protect the stock while you fit the pad to it. You may need to smooth the end of the stock with a rasp and sandpaper to remove all saw-tooth marks from the butt.

Once the butt is smoothed, seal the wood with some type of waterproof finish, and you're ready to place the buttpad on it. Carefully measure where the screw holes need to be and drill them into the stock. Do *not* try to force the screws into the stock without drilling holes; it won't work well and it's likely to crack the stock even if the screws should happen to be centered properly.

Most buttpads have a "hidden" screw hole these days; the screw and screwdriver are gently shoved through the rubber, which then seals over the screw after the screwdriver is pulled out. This looks neat and also holds the screws in place so they won't rattle loose as the Mini-14 is fired.

After tightening the screws and removing the screwdriver, your next task is to shape the pad since it will undoubted-ly overlap the edges of the stock. This shaping is done with a wood rasp or large-tooth file. Use sandpaper or a fine-tooth file for a smooth finish that matches the pad's unworked sur-face.

You'll need to experiment a bit to ascertain which tool works best on the pad you're shaping. The "right" tool varies with the pad. You might also discover that some pads have a definite grain you'll have to work with in order to achieve a smooth finish. As you finish your work, be sure to keep the tape protecting the stock in place; if you are care-ful, you can keep from scratching the stock so it won't need any refinishing.

There are a number of companies that offer recoil pads. Possibly the best pads are Uncle Mike's, which are available in many gun stores (or can be ordered by mail). In addition to a variety of thicknesses, colors (black or brown), and styles, Uncle Mike's offers black recoil pad spacers that can be used to match the length of pull to your measurements even more exactly (or allow you to lengthen the pull slightly later on). These spacers are 0.20 inches thick and are sold in packs of six for $14.

Uncle Mike's $12 Solid Recoil Pad (stock #50022 in brown or #50012 in black) will add half an inch to the length of pull; with the low recoil of the Mini-14, this pad's lack of cushioning will not present a problem. Uncle Mike's Open Cushion Recoil Pad ($13) will add 0.85 inches to the length of pull, and the Magnum ($15) and Ultra Mag ($20) pads each add an inch. (These also reduce felt recoil, which some people may find desirable with the Mini-30.)

Rubber recoil pads provide extra protection to the stock of the rifle if the Mini-14 is inadvertently dropped or slammed against a hard surface stock-first. Additionally, the pads help keep the rifle in place on the shoulder since the rubberized material tends to "grab" the fabric of a shirt or coat.

For those who want to add to the length of pull without cutting the stock, Choate Machine & Tool offers an extended buttpad for $15 that ads an inch to the stock. This is easy to mount: just unscrew the plastic buttplate and screw the Choate unit on.

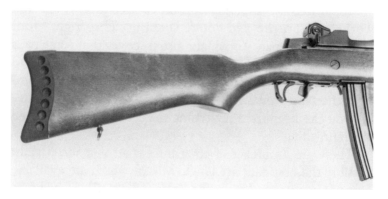

The Choate buttpad can be mounted onto the standard Mini-14 without having to cut the stock. It adds 1 inch to the length of pull, as well as maintaining the curve of the butt. (Photo courtesy of Choate Machine & Tool.)

The length of pull on some aftermarket folding stocks can also be changed. On the Ruger folding stock, as well as early Ruger look-alikes made by Ram-Line and manufactured by Falcon, length of pull isn't easily changed. Changing it entails cutting the metal rod of the stock or other extensive modifications; furthermore, the Ruger folders are currently limited to law-enforcement sales, so the few that were sold to the general public in the late 1980s have become collector's items. All in all, you'd be smarter to sell a Ruger stock, pocket the money, and then use some of it to purchase an aftermarket stock (or trade off a Falcon or old-style Ram-Line stock if it doesn't have the length of pull you need).

The most easily modified (and among the lightest) folding stocks are the plastic ones offered by Ram-Line for $63.

The Ruger-made folding stock folded (left) and open (right). Currently, it is also somewhat of a collector's item. Therefore, readers are advised to trade off the stock and purchase a more easily modified folder if the length of pull doesn't suit them. (Photo courtesy of Sturm, Ruger & Company.)

These futuristic-looking folders are almost all plastic, and their plastic buttplates can be removed by simply taking out a couple of screws. This instantly takes an inch off the length of pull. The do-it-yourselfer can easily create plastic or wooden spacers to go between the buttpad and stock in order to increase the length of pull. Black paint can be sprayed onto the spacers so they match the stock.

The most easily modified (and among the lightest) folding stocks are the plastic ones offered by Ram-Line. These futuristic-looking folders are almost all plastic, and their buttplates can be removed by taking out a couple of screws. (Photo courtesy of Ram-Line.)

Choate's plastic and metal folding stocks ($67) as well as their fixed plastic stocks ($45) can also be modified by removing or cutting their rubber buttpads or by adding longer pads and spacers to them. This cannot, however, be done to Choate's less-expensive ($49) folder made of ABS. With this unit, you'll have to carefully saw the stock to length and add a pad to it or file the butt flat so a pad can be added to lengthen the pull.

The purpose of the folding stock is to allow the rifle to be stored in a small space. Unfortunately, many people wish to maintain the short configuration of the rifle when it's actually being fired and do this by leaving the stock folded. The end result is extremely poor accuracy (unlike in the movies where everyone seems to fire weapons from the hip and hit their target). Don't be tempted to leave a folding stock in its

short position when you carry your Mini-14. Have the stock extended and shoulder the rifle so you'll hit your target.

If you need a short, compact rifle, there are several ways to achieve this without sacrificing accuracy. One is to shorten the barrel, and a simple way to do this is to remove the flash hider (if your Mini-14 has one). Since most Mini-14s are never fired in anger, or at least not in a situation where there will be return fire once a single antagonist is downed, chances are good that you'll never miss the flash hider. Removing it is a quick way to take an inch or more off the rifle's overall length.

It's also possible to shorten the barrel further, and it is not that hard to do, provided you take the time to do it right. Your first consideration must be the legal limits of barrel length, however. Otherwise, you may end up with an illegal weapon that will get you into trouble and be confiscated to boot. Unless you've

Choate's folding stock is easily modified and can serve as the basis of many super systems. Note flash hider, handguard, and bayonet lug, all offered by Choate. (Photo courtesy of Choate Machine & Tool.)

Folding stocks are ideal for storing the Mini-14 in a small space. The rifle should be fired with the stock extended, however, for maximum control and accuracy.

gone through some legal red tape and gotten governmental permission, the shortest legal barrel length on a rifle in the United States is sixteen inches. (And this may be too short for more backward municipalities, so be sure to check your local and state laws if you have any doubts.)

Barrel length is measured from the face of the bolt (when it's in battery) to the muzzle end of the rifle. The entire bore doesn't have to be rifled; for example, if the flash hider is welded onto the barrel it will be included in the overall length. This is handy for those needing a short barrel *and* a flash hider since the barrel can be cut shorter than sixteen inches and the hider welded to it for a 16-inch overall barrel length. If the flash hider is removable, however, then the length of the barrel is measured *without* the flash hider in place. To take your measurement, use a cleaning rod with the bolt of the Mini-14 in its forward, closed position. Take several measurements to be sure you have the right length. (On most factory Mini-14s, the barrel length is 18.5 inches, but measure to be sure.)

It's advisable to leave an extra 1/4 inch on a barrel when shortening it. This gives you room for error, takes care of the 1/16 inch of barrel that's lost in the saw cut, and gives you a little extra leeway with law-enforcement personnel who might measure the barrel later on. You'll never notice the extra 3/16 inch on the barrel, and it may serve as useful "legal insurance" in the near future. Also, if you mess up on the initial cut or if the muzzle gets dinged so it needs to be smoothed, the extra 3/16 inch will allow you a chance to redress the problem rather than having to get your Mini-14 rebarreled.

Measure the barrel and determine the amount you wish to remove. Assuming you have the standard 18.5-inch barrel, you'll probably want to lop 2 1/4 inches from it (or more if you'll be welding a flash hider or if you're doing the work for a legal entity, such as military or law-enforcement personnel).

In theory, the Mini-14 barrel could be shortened to eleven inches. But in practice, that's too short; the powder coming from the barrel is still burning, so it creates quite a fireball at the end of the muzzle. Also, the noise of the muzzle blast will be excessive and the velocity of the bullet rather low. Compounding problems, the gas system may not function reliably. Consequently, the shortest *practical* length for the Mini-14 barrel is thirteen inches (the length used with the AC-556 versions of the Mini-14 offered by Sturm, Ruger & Company). Don't be tempted to go shorter than that, even if you legally can.

Before you prepare to cut the barrel of the Mini-14, you'll need to take off its front sight (as outlined elsewhere in this book). Before doing so, be sure to mark the barrel so you can align the sight properly when you remount it. It's best to use a punch or sharp tool to make "witness" marks on the sight and barrel so you can realign the sight to within a fraction of an inch of where it was before, allowing the rear sight adjustments to rezero it easily. Needless to say, you should be sure to mark the portion of the barrel that you will *not* be sawing off. A straightedge is ideal for this work.

When you decide how much barrel to remove, carefully measure and mark the points at which you'll make your cut. Do this four times along opposite points on the circumference of the barrel. Rotate the barrel after you've finished making your marks to be sure all four are equidistant from the muzzle.

Masking tape or packing tape should be wrapped around the barrel carefully with the majority on the breech side of the marks. The tape will help you keep your cut straight and protect the remaining portion of the barrel from saw marks.

The barrel can be cut with the Mini-14 assembled, but it's easier if the stock and bolt are removed from the receiver/barrel assembly. Before cutting, push a dry cleaning patch into the barrel and leave it just short (on the breech side) of the point where the cut will be made. This will help keep metal filings out of the barrel and will simplify your cleaning chores after the cut is made.

Use a fine triangular file to cut a notch into the barrel, carefully copying one of your measurement marks. This file cut will create a starting point for the hacksaw. Before you start working with the saw, it's prudent to secure the barrel in a vise so it won't wander around. For the best cut, place a very fine blade on the hacksaw; this will take longer but will make the cut fine enough that polishing the muzzle crown will take minimal time and effort.

Start the hacksaw cut at the file mark. Make a shallow initial cut and extend it around the circumference of the barrel, taking care not to go through to the bore. Be sure to use the tape as a guide. You'll need to remove the Mini-14 from the vise from time to time to rotate it slightly and continue the cut around the barrel. By ringing the barrel and slowly deepening the cut, you'll keep the cut square around the barrel and be less apt to damage the bore.

When the barrel is finally sawed off, leave the tape in place. Push the dry patch toward the new muzzle until it rests just below the new barrel's crown. Don't remove the patch yet; it can continue to catch metal filings.

Lightly polish the crown of the barrel with a fine file if there are any saw marks on it. Again, if you took care to ring the barrel and used a fine hacksaw blade, this work will be minimal.

A drill press or lathe can be used to countersink the bore. This will help keep the accuracy of the Mini-14 from being ruined should it get a "ding" on its crown. To countersink the bore, set the barrel in place and use a countersink tool or perhaps a triangular router bit to cut into the bore.

A triangular router can be found at most hardware stores; get a carbide one if possible, especially if you're countersinking a stainless barrel. Brownells offers a 79-degree Muzzle Crowning Cutter (#080-586-079) for $19, which can also be used. If you have a Dremel tool, you can use a ball stone in it and set the machine at a high speed to countersink the barrel

Crowning the muzzle is a little tricky. If you're not sure whether you can handle this, try your hand on the piece of barrel you've cut off. If the work goes smoothly, you're probably ready to tackle the barrel on your Mini-14. If you have troubles, cut off the barrel stub you removed and practice a little more. If you're still not sure you want to tackle the job, a gunsmith can do it for you for just a few dollars.

Polish the end of the muzzle with a fine file. If you want a mirror polish, you can use a Dremel tool with a mandrel to hold a square of emery paper and use light pressure to polish the front of the barrel. Or, if you don't own a Dremel tool, you can glue a square of emery paper on a large piece of doweling and mount it in a power drill or drill press. Set the machine at a high speed and again, use light pressure. Take care to keep the angle of the dowel and barrel the same so the emery hits the muzzle squarely.

If you're working on a stainless-steel barrel, you're now finished. Blued barrels can have the muzzle left "in the white" or can be darkened with cold blueing chemicals (available in most gun stores). You can then remount your front sight or add a flash hider with a sight on it.

If you've driven off the front sight assembly, you'll probably need to smooth the burrs on its rear side with a file before remounting it. Drive it back onto the barrel and check to be sure it's square. Once it's in position, use a small drill bit to cut a notch for the roll pin that secures the sight. Drift in the roll pin. With a blued sight, you'll need to use some touch-up blue to complete your job.

If you're cutting a barrel shorter than sixteen inches so a flash hider can be used to bring it back to the legal length, the hider must be permanently attached to the barrel. In the past, flash hiders were attached with soft solder, but this isn't very practical since soft solder can melt if your barrel becomes overheated with extended shooting. The flash hider then drops off or, worse yet, is struck by a bullet exiting the muzzle. A better, safer bet is to use silver solder or to weld the flash hider in place.

This same technique could be used to create a pistol version of the Mini-14. Since the recoil system of the Mini-14 is located under the barrel, it's simple to purchase a pistol-grip stock, lop off the stock from the pistol grip back, and then shorten the Mini-14's barrel to thirteen inches, and you'll have what is popularly called an "assault pistol."

While creating a pistol from a Mini-14 is simple, keeping everything legal isn't. Transforming a rifle into a pistol is illegal unless you first get permission from the Bureau of Alcohol, Tobacco, and Firearms (BATF), get the proper paperwork squared away, pass the fingerprint test, and pay your $200 tax. And even then, you can't create such a sawed-off rifle in many parts of the United States legally unless you're doing it for a government agency. (Failure to get legal permission beforehand is a good way to face stiff fines and time in prison.)

The situation would change if a new receiver and new parts that had never been assembled as a rifle were used to create a pistol. Then the work could be done with little red tape, other than registering the receiver as a firearm. But new, unassembled receivers and other parts for the Mini-14 are not available in the marketplace. Consequently, creating a pistol version of the Mini-14 isn't practical for most of us from a legal standpoint.

An easier way to obtain a shorter package for the Mini-14 is to mount a bullpup stock on it. The bullpup stock places the rear of the receiver near the buttplate with a pistol grip and trigger group ahead of the magazine. This design reduces the overall length of a rifle with a standard barrel by ten inches. It has the added benefit of keeping the barrel long, so there's no loss of bullet velocity or increase in muzzle noise and flash.

The bullpup design is not without its shortcomings. Trigger pull becomes less precise due to the mechanical linkage involved. Also, left-handed holds are dangerous because the empty brass will be ejected toward the shooter (and the operating lever will hit him in the face). And the shooter's face is positioned over the receiver, increasing the amount of mechanical noise he'll hear and adding a bit of risk as well since a malfunction that causes failure of the bolt or a premature ignition of the round is more likely to injure him. Despite these shortcomings, many people elect to use the bullpup design, especially military users traveling in armored vehicles (as witnessed by the popularity of the German G11, Britain's L70 Enfield, the Steyr AUG, and the French FAMAS, as well as the Valmet M82 and

Chinese bullpup versions of the AK-47).

For a time, many hobbyists and a few small businesses experimented with modifying the Mini-14 into a bullpup configuration. These designs were generally a bit crude, but effective. The modifications were usually done by chopping the stock off the Mini-14 just behind the receiver and then cutting the butt end of the gun so it could be glued to the cut-down stock. A portion was then used to cover the trigger with the safety left exposed at the front of the trigger guard.

The inside of the stock was then carved out to allow a metal rod to operate inside it. This rod (or rods) extended back along the side of the magazine well to engage the trigger (the receiver was then enclosed). The forward end of the rod then was connected to a new trigger located under what had been the forearm of the rifle. A pistol grip was attached to the underside of the forearm and a new trigger guard added.

The bullpup created this way dictated a new sighting arrangement since the cheek rested over the rear sight. This usually meant an AR-15-style carrying handle was attached to the upper receiver of the Mini-14. When all was said and done, most of these designs had a rather cobbled look (something that can be said of most bullpups), and often the sighting system was not as accurate as one might hope.

For experimenters, there are other possible bullpup arrangements. One would be to use the extended 20- or 30-round magazine of the rifle for the pistol grip. While this creates a rather hefty grip, it does work and leaves the shooter with the magazine in hand, ready for quick exchanges.

It's also possible to extend the length of pull of a bullpup by elongating the stock behind the receiver slightly. While this would seem to create a rather uncomfortable hold, it doesn't, because the pistol grip can be held with two hands (similar to the hold used by most pistol shooters these days). The big advantage of this arrangement is that it places the

An extended-length-of-pull bullpup with an elongated stock behind the receiver. A two-handed "pistol hold" makes this a comfortable way to shoot. Big advantages of this design: it allows standard sights to be used, and it puts the shooter's face farther from the receiver in case a cartridge should fail.

shooter's face farther back so the sights on the rifle can be used without adding higher AR-15-style sights. Additionally, the shooter's face is off the receiver, which might prevent a serious accident if a cartridge should fail to function properly.

A third bullpup variation would be to place the rifle over—rather than against—the shoulder, with the magazine behind the shooter and the pistol grip nearly at the front of the barrel. This odd arrangement has several distinct advantages. Foremost is the fact that the weight of the rifle is nearly balanced so it can remain comfortably shouldered and ready to fire for long periods of time. A second plus is that the forward pistol grip gives greater control of the rifle during recoil.

On the minus side, this bullpup arrangement necessitates a new sighting system, which also has a rather short sighting

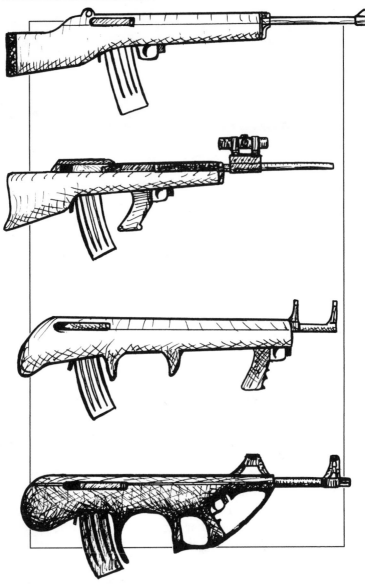

Sketches of possible bullpup layouts. The top rifle uses the magazine for a grip. The second from top is a standard bullpup (with a scope mount rather than iron sights). The lower two guns are over-the-shoulder bullpups; inverted horns go on either side of the shoulder. The bottom version places the pistol grip at an angle for a comfortable hold.

plane. Additionally, the magazine is awkward to replace during reloading (the rifle must be rotated so the barrel points upward, or the firearm must be removed from the shoulder altogether).

The most practical way to create a bullpup configuration for the Mini-14 is to simply purchase one of the recently introduced Muzzlelite series of bullpup kits. These stocks are well designed, both functionally and aesthetically. Rather than modifying an existing stock, you fasten the kit's two plastic half shells around the receiver and barrel of a Mini-14 after removing its original stock. In addition to having iron sights incorporated into a handy carrying handle, the shell also accommodates a scope mount (which comes with the kit).

About the only quarrel shooters may have with the Muzzlelite kit will be with the trigger. It's a little short, so you may find it doesn't feel very comfortable. This can be cured, however, by simply cutting a metal trigger shoe and gluing or screwing it onto the trigger.

An additional, though minor, shortcoming is that the shell has to be removed to thoroughly clean the rifle. This isn't too much of a problem, however, and modern cleaning sprays (like Outers Crud Cutter) make it possible to carry out many cleaning chores without disassembling the Muzzlelite shell.

At $97, the Muzzlelite kit is the perfect solution for those needing a bullpup version of the Mini-14. Best of all, kits are also available for the 10/22, the Marlin Camp Rifles, and other guns, so that the owner of the Mini-14 can create a "family" of bullpup rifles that are all operated in a similar manner.

One important point: take care *not* to shorten the barrel of a rifle being used in a bullpup. This is because shortening the Mini-14's (or other rifle's) barrel to 16 inches often will result in a gun with an *overall* length below the 26-inch legal minimum. So if you're going to use a bullpup stock, take advantage of the ability to create a short package *without* needing to shorten the barrel. This will allow you to stay on the safe side of the law.

The importance of using quality ammunition and keeping the Mini-14 in proper working order when it's in the bullpup configuration cannot be emphasized enough. One premature firing of a shell because of a protruding primer, one too-powerful load in a cartridge, one bullet stuck in the barrel when another cartridge is fired . . . and you'll suffer a serious accident, with your face in the area where the "action" will be taking place. Don't take any chances. Use quality ammunition—cannelured bullets if possible—whenever you're firing a bullpup.

Whether bullpup or standard configuration, the plus of many aftermarket stocks is their pistol grip. With an extended magazine (on a non-bullpup), the shooter can obtain a very secure hold by exerting pressure against the side of the magazine with the off arm while firmly holding the pistol grip. The pistol grip gives greater control and steadiness than can be realized with the conventional "sporter" stock normally found on the Mini-14.

If you wish to add a pistol grip to a regular Mini-14 stock "on the cheap," it's quite simple to do so. All you need is an AR-15 grip, which can be purchased from a supplier like Ram-Line or SGW and is easy to fit to the Mini-14 or Mini-30.

Adding a pistol grip to your standard rifle stock has the side effect of increasing the length of pull by about an inch. This may enable you to avoid having to lengthen the pull or facilitate cutting the stock off straight and adding a recoil pad, if the curved buttplate of the Mini-14 isn't to your liking. (It will also necessitate some changes if the stock was "just right" the way it was—a definite negative to this procedure.)

In order to accommodate the AR-15 pistol grip to the Mini-14 stock, it's necessary for the grip to point downward at a greater angle than it normally does on the AR-15 or on the Mini-14s that have pistol-grip stocks. This is necessary because the wood in the stock where the grip is attached is quite narrow. Removing enough wood for a standard grip angle would weaken the stock to the point that it would break easily if too much stress were placed on it. Fortunately, this steeper grip angle is quite comfortable. (For those who wish to have the standard grip angle, it will be necessary to cut out a square at the top of the stock's regular grip area and glue in a piece of wood, using the techniques outlined below for building a higher cheek rest.)

The actual procedure of mounting the grip is pretty straightforward. After you place the grip on the stock, draw around the grip with a pencil. Then chisel out the wood where the grip will rest, carving out about an eighth of an inch. Next, drill a new hole in the AR-15 grip (behind the one it already has). This will enable you to fasten the grip in place without running a screw too close to the trigger mechanism of the Mini-14.

Before fastening the pistol grip in place, you need to determine how much wood to remove from the stock immediately to the rear of the grip in order to allow a comfortable hold. The less wood you remove the better, but some will have to be taken out. Remove the material with a wood rasp and then use sandpaper to smooth everything once the shaping is completed.

Once the wood is removed, you may wish to use paint stripper on the stock, then restain and refinish it after your work is done so your modification will look good. Then you can drill a small hole for the screw that will hold the pistol grip in place (use the grip as a guide for the hole's position).

A lock washer is a good idea to help hold the pistol grip in place. The small depression chiseled into the stock will help keep the grip from rotating, so just one screw will secure the pistol grip. If you have the few tools needed to complete this job, you'll be able to create an attractive, functional pistol-grip stock for just a few dollars spent on the AR-15 grip.

Whether do-it-yourself or aftermarket, a pistol-grip stock without finger swells on it may cause a shooter's trigger-finger hand to slide up on the pistol grip after the gun is held for any length of time. Although this isn't much of a handicap, it can be irritating.

A quick fix with older stocks using a removable AR-15 grip is to purchase a new A2-style grip from Ram-Line, SGW, L.L. Baston, or one of the other companies offering the grips (for around $8) and replace it. These A2 replacement grips have finger swells that help keep the fingers in place; the wide grooves in the back of most of these also help you hold onto the grip.

The new A2 grip is simple to mount. You remove the screw from the inside of the old grip (reached through the bottom hole in the grip), slide the grip off, put the new A2 grip on, and replace the screw and its washer. Take care to tighten the screw so it won't shake loose. While older grips (as well as the new Colt A2 grip) are open on the bottom, most A2 grips have a trap door in them. In addition to being useful for storing odds and ends, the trap door keeps the grip from getting filled with dirt or mud.

If the pistol grip is molded to the stock so it is one solid piece, or if you'd prefer not to spend even five bucks to add finger swells, it's a minor do-it-yourself job to modify it into a finger-swell grip.

To create a finger swell, drill a small hole where the protrusion should be and add a small screw. Screw it only partway into the hole so there is space between the underside of the screw head and the grip. Place epoxy putty around the screw where the swell belongs. Once the putty has hardened, you can shape and smooth it with a file; grooves, checkering, or stippling can be cut into the front and/or rear of the grip with a file or hacksaw blade for an even more secure grip.

There's no need to limit yourself to one finger swell. You may wish to create one for between your middle and ring fingers and a second for between your ring and little fingers. Spray paint can be utilized to give your "new" grip a uniform color when it's finished.

One important feature of aftermarket plastic stocks is their ability to resist abuse and moisture. This often makes them more desirable than wooden stocks in areas that have high humidity, lots of rain or snow, or are near bodies of water. And, as an added benefit, the pistol grip of most of these stocks gives the shooter better control of the Mini-14.

Whether you go with the pistol grip modification of the Mini-14's wooden stock or simply keep it as is, it's smart to coat the inside of the stock with a material that will help it resist absorbing moisture. Not only will this protect the wood, it will prevent swelling, which can reduce accuracy by causing the point of aim to wander according to weather conditions. Linseed oil is the traditional material for this, but you'll often get good results with a flat polyurethane, which is easier to work into the wood.

Placement of the swivels on the stock and lower gas block (under the barrel) are fine for the over-the-shoulder carry of the Mini-14 with a sling. Such a carry becomes a bit awkward with 30- or 40-round magazines, however, and the shooter can't bring the rifle into action nearly as fast as when it's carried in the "assault" position (at the hip). Consequently, when it comes time to carry a Mini-14 in the field, many shooters will find a quick modification of the swivel placement on the stock (or to the sling) to be a real asset.

Changing the position of the rear swivel is simple: you merely unscrew it, drill a hole at the new position for the swivel, and screw it into place. While moving the swivel to the top rear of the stock (perhaps replacing the top buttplate screw) seems most ideal for the assault carry, this actually causes the sling to wrap around your shoulder when you bring the rifle up, and to get in the way of the buttplate as well. Consequently, placing the swivel on the side of the stock is generally more satisfactory. Be sure to shoulder the rifle a few times before drilling any screw holes to avoid mounting the swivel where your cheek rests on the stock.

Once the swivel is repositioned on the stock, all you need is a long sling, or you can add a long shoelace to a standard sling. The rear of the sling is looped through the newly positioned swivel on the side of the stock, and the shoelace or front of the sling is attached to the front swivel and draped over the side of the forearm. A little practice will enable you to quickly bring the rifle to your shoulder for accurate shots and—for those who insist on firing inaccurately—it's also possible to fire from the hip without raising the rifle as it hangs on the sling.

For those who don't wish to reposition the swivel on the stock, there's an even simpler solution that will enable the Mini-14 to be carried in the assault position. Simply use a pair of long shoelaces, looping one through the rear swivel so either side of the lace comes up alongside the stock. Then fasten the two ends of the shoelace to the tail end of the sling. The second shoelace goes into the front swivel in a similar manner so each side of it comes up on either side of the foregrip. Provided the laces are kept very loose, they'll slide over the back of the buttplate or drop to the side when the rifle is shouldered.

Of course many shooters prefer to carry their rifles and not fool with slings. But then the swivels often clatter, making an irritating noise that can scare game or give away your position if you're using the Mini-14 to defend yourself. Therefore, for such shooters, the swivels are best removed.

The rear swivel is simple to remove—just unscrew it using a screwdriver in the loop of the swivel as a lever. The front swivel is more difficult. Use a pair of screwdrivers to bend the two ends of the swivel out of their mount in the base of the lower gas block. Once you get one of the ends bent out, then you can slide the swivel out of the gas block. Save both swivels so you can replace them if you wish to sell your rifle later or place a sling on it.

If you have a plastic stock on your Mini-14, you can shorten the assault carry sling considerably by placing a new swivel on the side of the stock about even with the front of the receiver. All you'll need is a sling swivel (available at most gun stores for just a few dollars).

To mount the swivel, remove the stock from the rifle and pick the spot for the new swivel. Select a location on the stock where the plastic is pretty thick. If the swivel screw is too long, cut it to length with a file or hacksaw. Once everything is right, drill a small hole in the stock and screw the swivel in. Now the front of the sling will be closer to your body, where it's less apt to get snagged on branches.

An alternative to the assault carry is the German G3-style carry. For this, you need to move the sling swivel at the rear of the stock to its side, and you'll also need a six-foot-long sling. In order to work, the sling must have a slide fastener at each of its ends and a third slide fastener—with the sling threaded through just one of its openings—in the middle of the sling. One end of the sling is fastened to the front swivel of the Mini-14. The sling is then looped through the side-mounted rear swivel and brought forward again toward the front of the rifle, where it's looped through the open half of the third sling fastener that's riding free on the sling, and fastened.

With this arrangement, the outside loop of the sling goes around your back and over the left shoulder (assuming you're right-handed), while the half of the sling next to the

Mini-14 goes in front of your chest.

When worn this way, the rifle can be brought into a port-arms position, where it will be held tightly in place by the sling. It can also be quickly pushed into assault position, shoved into an at-the-hips position, thrust up to ride behind your back, or brought to the shoulder—all without changing the adjustment on the sling—and with the rifle held there until you change positions again.

For those who wish to have a "sporter" rifle sometimes and a "military" rifle at other times, it's simple to purchase an aftermarket folding stock and the hardware (forearm liner, stock reinforcement insert, and the two screws and washers for the insert) from Sturm, Ruger & Company. By adding the hardware to the aftermarket stock, you can exchange one stock for the other in a matter of minutes. All you need to do is pull out the trigger guard (as you would when field-stripping the rifle), then remove the trigger group and receiver/barrel assembly, put them into the second stock, and snap the trigger guard shut in the new stock. This takes only a few seconds once you get the hang of it.

Those wishing to use the Mini-14 for self-defense find a bullpup stock makes the gun considerably more maneuverable. Shown here is a stainless Mini-14 with a Muzzlelite stock, an Eagle 35-round magazine, and a Choate flash hider.

Those wishing to use the Mini-14 for self-defense in an urban area—possibly even indoors—will find that a 16-inch barrel or bullpup stock make the gun considerably more maneuverable in hallways. The shorter length also makes the Mini-14 less apt to be snatched by someone hiding in the darkness.

In the past, the catch to using the .223 Remington cartridge for indoor combat was that the bullet would penetrate building materials. This meant that the homeowner or police officer had to use either a pistol or a carbine firing a pistol round, or else risk having a .223 bullet strike an innocent bystander who is out of sight behind a wall or some such thing. This situation has changed, however, thanks to a new round introduced by the Federal Cartridge Company. The new cartridge is sold under the trade name Blitz or Varmint (product #223D).

The Blitz has a 40-grain bullet that leaves the barrel at more than three hundred fps (feet per second) faster than the standard .223 bullet. This faster speed, coupled with the bullet's hollow-point, thin-jacketed design, causes it to shatter on impact. The Blitz will penetrate many materials less than a hollow-point 9mm Luger bullet would, making it ideal for self-defense even in urban areas.

Ballistic tests with the Blitz show that when a 1-in-7 twist is used with the new Mini-14 rifles, the bullet disintegrates into more than a hundred fragments. When striking human flesh, each of these fragments cuts a separate channel, creating a shotgun-like wound with penetration up to nine inches. This is generally considered sufficient as a fight stopper while not being so excessive as to be overly dangerous to bystanders. So, while no round is harmless enough to make bystanders 100-percent safe if you're not careful enough to think before shooting, this round is as safe as any other, and safer than most. Consequently, the Blitz has become popular among many police forces that employ the Mini-14 or other .223 rifles.

Provided a little common sense is exercised, Federal's Blitz is certainly ideal for many indoor self-defense situations, especially with the faster twist of the new Mini-14s. Outdoors, the situation changes somewhat since the Blitz loses velocity more quickly than other, heavier .223 rounds. The cartridge is also a bit more prone to disintegration when it hits a branch or other obstacle. In general, however, this cartridge comes very close to being an "all-purpose" round for self-defense.

It should be noted that even with standard .223 bullets, there is some break-up with 1-in-12 or higher twists. Since the early Mini-14s had 1-in-10 twists and the newer ones have 1-in-7 twists, they are much deadlier than might otherwise be the case. Such fast twists are very deadly, causing even standard FMJ (full-metal jacket) bullets to fragment into several pieces on impact with flesh-and-blood targets. Given the effective range of the .223 (to three hundred yards or more—some people are able to engage targets at six hundred yards with a scoped rifle and suitable terrain), the Mini-14 makes a very potent weapon.

Anyone who has to carry a Mini-14 for any length of time will appreciate its light weight. There are ways to make it even lighter, however. One simple way is to minimize the amount of ammunition in the rifle. With a .223 cartridge weighing in at about half an ounce, a loaded 40-round magazine hanging in a Mini-14 is going to make it almost a pound heavier than the same gun with a 5-round magazine in place.

Your Mini-14 may also have some hardware on it that's not needed and can be removed easily. For example, if you're using a scope on your rifle, then taking off the rear and front sights (and perhaps even grinding off the sight assembly on the standard Mini-14 receiver) will lighten the rifle noticeably—and give it cleaner lines to boot. Flash hiders, swivels,

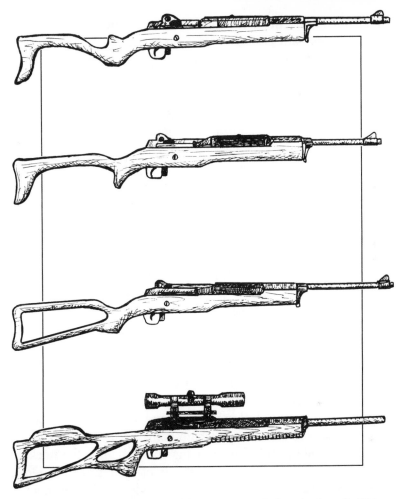

For weight reduction, it's possible to create a skeletonized stock. This can be done with a drill, saw, rasps, and sandpaper. Such modifications can create a very attractive, one-of-a-kind firearm. The lower version is created by adding wood to the stock before skeletonization.

or other features can often be removed as well without any loss of capability.

Except for the Ram-Line stocks, most folders add more than a pound to the Mini-14; avoiding them will greatly reduce the weight of the gun. Buying a blued rather than stainless gun will also give you a bit less to lug about. More weight can be eliminated by shortening the barrel.

It's also possible to reduce the diameter of the Mini-14 or Mini-30 barrel, especially toward the muzzle end. This work is better left to a very skilled gunsmith, however, since it calls for lathe work, and measurements must be very accurate if the barrel is to remain safe.

It's also practical to reduce the weight of the standard wooden stocks. To do this, simply remove the buttplate and use a power drill and small wooden drill bits to carve out the wood on the inside of the stock. Provided you take a little care not to go clear through to the outside of the stock, you can hollow it out and thereby reduce its weight. This could also serve as a makeshift storage compartment, though carrying anything in it would defeat the purpose of reducing the rifle's weight. For minimal weight, you should keep the standard buttplate on the rifle if possible and avoid using recoil pads or stock extension pads, since these can add considerable weight to the Mini-14.

For even greater weight reduction, it's possible to create a skeletonized version of either a plastic or wooden stock. This can be done with a drill, saw, rasps, and sandpaper. Provided care is taken to round off all sharp corners with the rasp and sand the final finish before stripping and restaining the stock, this can create a very attractive, one-of-a-kind firearm. Do remember that such a stock will be considerably weaker than it originally was; don't abuse it or it's likely to break.

For those wishing to create a really fancy two-toned gun, it's possible to buy a stainless or blued trigger group that contrasts with the finish of the gun you own. If you own a stainless and blued gun or know someone who is willing to swap parts with you, then you can "mix and match" parts to your heart's content. The end results can be rakish, though they may appeal to some people.

With such exchanges, it is important to exercise caution with the bolt, which *must* be checked for proper head spacing. Simply exchanging the bolt assembly from one gun to the other will sometimes create a dangerous situation, so if you wish to switch two such assemblies, be sure to have a gunsmith check both guns for safety so you won't be shopping for a new face after firing your mix-and-match creations.

It's also possible to "engine-turn" exposed parts of the Mini-14 or Mini-30. This work can be especially attractive on the stainless versions and will improve the lubrication on either a blued or stainless gun. Engine-turning (also known as "jeweling") is done by spinning abrasive discs or brushes on metal to create a swirling pattern. These decorative patterns generally cover the surface of metal parts of firearms in overlapping groups. They also help smooth the action of the gun by retaining oil on their surfaces so the metal actually glides on a thin film of oil.

Drill presses are nearly essential for jeweling, and it's a good idea to develop some skill by practicing on scrap steel before tackling a firearm. For do-it-yourself jeweling, a new pencil can be cut in two and mounted in a drill press chuck so that the rubber eraser points downward. Next, a small disc of abrasive cloth (100-grit or finer) is cut and glued to the eraser. Start by lowering the spinning cloth disc onto the surface of the metal for just a moment.

Another method of jeweling is to use a pen with an ink eraser on its top. Cut the eraser flat (and cut it again as the work progresses and its edges start to wear). The eraser is spun in the press to touch the metal and create the jeweled pattern.

Of course, really professional jeweling is done with brushes and grit. If you choose to go this route, the jeweling brush and compound are available from B-Square for just a few dollars.

To do the actual jeweling, the piece you're working on should be clamped to the drill press table and the motor of the press placed on a high speed. The bit or brush touches the metal for just an instant to create a single swirl on the metal's surface. The piece is then shifted slightly to one side and another pattern made the same way. When you're doing this work, keep patterns in a straight line, with the swirls just touching at their edges or barely overlapping. Care should be taken to keep the pattern symmetrical and consistent.

Due to the improved lubrication offered by jeweling, the Mini-14/Mini-30 trigger group can benefit especially from the process. (For the steps necessary to disassemble the trigger group and all other parts, get my book *The Mini-14: The Plinker, Hunter, Assault, and Everything Else Rifle*, available from Paladin Press.) Other areas that could be jeweled include the bolt, receiver, or almost any other metal part.

The main thing to remember in making any modifications to your Mini-14 or Mini-30 is not to get carried away and to be sure you really need to have the work done before tackling it. Otherwise, you'll create a really gaudy and/or awkward firearm that may attract more catcalls than compliments and, in any event, won't be much fun to shoot.

CHAPTER 3

Creating a Superaccurate Mini-14

Most people purchase the Mini-14 or Mini-30 for defense or for hunting, and the rifles fulfill these jobs very nicely. For the most part, however, these rifles are not tack drivers. Often groups as large as four inches at one hundred yards are about the best some of these guns can do. While this can hardly be considered poor in terms of hunting rifles or military arms, it isn't good for target shooting, varminting, or sniping, which call for a high degree of precision.

Of course, some of these rifles are a bit more accurate than others, and the newer guns tend to have greater accuracy than the older ones. The best route is sometimes to try several guns and keep the Mini-14 that outperforms the others. But there are also ways you can increase the accuracy of any of these rifles.

One quick fix is to purchase a plastic stock for the Mini-14 or Mini-30. Often, these stocks will cut groups in half since they are less apt to warp and appear to give better support to the rifle. And for those who aren't interested in military-looking pistol-grip stocks, Choate Machine and Tool now offers a $45 fiberglass-filled plastic stock that has the same lines as the standard wooden stock that comes with most Mini-14s.

Another thing that *may* reduce the size of groups is scoping the rifle. This isn't the cure-all some would think. Surprisingly enough, a scope often doesn't reduce the size of a group being fired, but it does help you pick out your target more precisely. For some shooters it can help reduce group sizes by drawing attention to the rifle's movement when it is held "steady."

Inside sources say Sturm, Ruger & Company has considered introducing a "heavy-barrel" varmint version of the Mini-14. Should this become available, it would certainly be a quick way to obtain an accurate off-the-shelf Mini-14.

For those wanting to modify a standard Mini-14 into a heavy-barrel configuration, it's best to have the work done by a professional gunsmith. Removing the barrel on a Mini-14 is not an easy task, and some modification to the gas system will be necessary due to the new dimensions of the barrel. A number of companies offer highly accurate barrels that might be placed on the Mini-14; Douglas barrels have a very good reputation for accuracy and would be the first choice for most shooters.

If you can't find a local gunsmith to do the work, Accuracy Rifle Systems will handle the work by mail. Be sure to contact the company before sending your rifle; get a firm quote on prices and the procedure of sending a gun to them via United Parcel Service (UPS). Currently, the company guarantees one Minute of Angle (MOA) accuracy on the Mini-14s they work on, which translates to 1-inch groups at 100 yards—given good ammunition, a firm shooting rest, and shooting skill on the part of the gunner.

A new barrel isn't always necessary to improve the Mini-14's accuracy. Sometimes a barrel will have nicks or burrs on

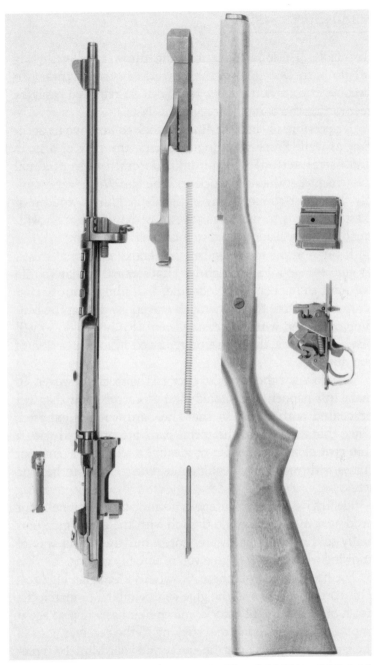

Do-it-yourselfers can glass-bed a stock. This field-stripped Mini-14 would have its stock glassed where the rear and lower edge of the receiver and trigger group normally touch it. (Photo courtesy of Sturm, Ruger & Company.)

its muzzle. These imperfections can throw a bullet slightly off its path as it leaves the barrel, causing accuracy to become erratic. Fortunately, these can be removed easily by recrowning the barrel. (More on this later.)

It's possible to "bed" a Mini-14 stock to improve its accuracy as well. Proper bedding (reducing the play of a stock and barrel action) will minimize lateral or longitudinal movement between the stock and the barrel/receiver assembly. The most common way of tightly bedding a wooden or plastic stock is to use some type of epoxy filler, often with small glass fibers added to it to increase its strength.

It's important to remember that epoxy is normally used to glue things together tightly. That's exactly what you do *not* want to happen with your rifle, so it's important to coat all metal surfaces that may touch the epoxy during the bedding operation with a releasing agent. Failure to do so will result in a stock that can't be removed from the action of the rifle!

You do want the epoxy to stick to the stock, however. To make this happen, you should sand down the areas that will be coated with epoxy so that the bare wood is exposed. Once that's done and the metal parts are protected with a thin coat of wax, oil, or (most ideally) a releasing agent that comes with most glass bedding kits, you're ready to bed the stock.

Ideally, you'll buy the epoxy formulated specifically for bedding a rifle. You can do the job with the epoxy glue normally sold at most hardware stores, but there's no way of knowing what quality of glue you're actually getting.

For best results, purchase Brownells' Acraglas kit ($8). This comes with dye so the glue can be mixed to match the finish of your Mini-14's stock, and the kit has a release agent to prevent the material from sticking to the receiver parts of the gun. Once you've got the epoxy and your Mini-14 is prepared, follow the directions for mixing the epoxy very carefully, observing all the instructions regarding hardening time and so forth.

The areas to be coated on the top of the stock are at the rear "U" where the rear of the receiver rests on the top edge of the stock, the inner areas where the receiver rests on the stock around the metal stock reinforcement insert, and the top edge of the stock where the receiver on either side of the bolt normally rests.

On the lower edge of the stock, you should add glass bedding to the area where the rear of the trigger group rests and to the edge of the stock where the bars on either side of the magazine well rest.

Once the epoxy is in place on the stock, very carefully assemble the rifle and allow the bedding to harden. Do not fully latch the trigger guard. Instead, leave a little clearance (1/4 inch to 1/8 inch) between it and its latch position. This will ensure a very tight fit after the epoxy dries and the trigger assembly is actually locked in place.

Before the epoxy bedding hardens, the excess glass compound that has been displaced along the outside of the action should be carefully removed from the stock and receiver with a small knife. Use a cloth moistened in acetone to remove the last smears of epoxy. Be sure to check the stock from time to time before the epoxy starts to harden to be sure it hasn't dripped onto the stock.

After the epoxy has hardened, the action of the rifle may be stuck to the epoxy. Provided you've coated the metal parts with a releasing agent, this is no problem. Simply tap the parts gently and they should come free. After the trigger group is out, you can usually free the barrel/receiver assembly by turning the Mini-14 upside down and tapping the butt end of the stock against the workbench top.

Be sure to examine the bedding after the action has been removed from it. The surface of the compound should show definite impressions of all the metal parts coming in contact with it. If you see any areas with large voids, sand down the surface, place a small amount of epoxy on it, and repeat the bedding process.

When the bedding is complete, examine the metal of the receiver, trigger group, and inside of the stock and carefully remove any excess epoxy that has oozed away and hardened in areas where it doesn't belong. This is best done with a very sharp knife or rasp. Be very careful not to disturb the bedded areas when removing excess epoxy.

If you're a little leery of using epoxy bedding, it's also possible to glue small shims of wood into the areas described above with wooden stocks. Plastic stocks can often be built up using the soldering iron and the plastic welding techniques outlined previously.

By slowly building such shims up, you can tighten the action/stock fit and thereby bed the rifle. But this takes a lot of time and the end result often isn't as good as epoxy bedding. It's also possible to create too tight a fit with shims so that accuracy actually suffers.

Surprisingly enough, the handguard over the Mini-14's barrel should have a little play in it. This keeps it from exerting pressure between the receiver and barrel if it expands due to heat or humidity. If it doesn't have a small amount of longitudinal play (from the front to rear axis), then you should sand down the front and rear faces of the handguard. Be sure to seal wooden handguards afterward so they won't swell when exposed to moisture.

For optimal accuracy, a Mini-14's wooden stock should be coated with a waterproof varnish. Be especially careful to coat all open-end grain cuts inside and outside of the stock. And remember to replace the coating as it wears off so the rifle doesn't lose its accuracy gradually.

Often a bedded Mini-14 will start firing with considerably more accuracy after twenty or more rounds have been put through it. This is because the action becomes more firmly seated in the stock after the gun has recoiled and cycled a number of times. Therefore, if accuracy is of prime importance, you should fire the rifle a bit before zeroing it or actually starting your target shooting.

Since clean barrels also often shoot more accurately than those that have had a number of rounds put down them, you may also wish to clean the barrel of a bedded gun without field-stripping it. Do be careful to keep the cleaning rod from rubbing against the muzzle area of the barrel since this can ruin its accuracy.

A point to consider: most firearms shoot so accurately that their owners can't take full advantage of their potential precision. So rather than spend a lot of money rebarreling or reworking your rifle, it's often smarter to do everything you can to make *yourself* as accurate a shooter as possible. There are a number of ways to do this.

Shooting from a rest has always been a good way to improve accuracy. While use of a rest doesn't actually improve the capabilities of the rifle, it does improve those of the shooter. A rest will steady the swaying created by breathing, blood pounding in the arteries, and the various tics and twitches of the human muscular system. Therefore, it is a must for really accurate shooting with a Mini-14.

Unfortunately, while a rest won't improve the capabilities of the Mini-14, it can hurt them. Leaning the gun's barrel over a branch or attaching a heavy bipod to the muzzle end of the barrel can cause enough barrel flex to create a slight change of zero between firing with and without the rest or bipod. Thus, a heavy bipod may cause the gun to shoot high when you're shooting from a standing position and a tad low when actually being used for prone shots.

The solution to this problem is simple: use a lightweight bipod and mount it to the forearm of the stock if possible (or at least as close as possible to the stock if it must go on the barrel). The three best bipods for the Mini-14 are Ram-

Line's lightweight nylon bipod, the Harris bipod, and Cherokee's stock-attached bipod. It's better to support the stock rather than the barrel of the gun, otherwise your rifle's accuracy can suffer to some extent.

If you're using a scope on your Mini-14, you should consider adding a cheek pad to your rifle to make sighting through it easier. Leather, cloth, or plastic pads can be improvised for the Mini-14 (one often sees strange contraptions on target guns created from tape, cardboard, and other unidentifiable materials).

Those using plastic-stocked rifles can even weld an improvised plastic cheek rest to their stock. Wooden stocks are nearly as flexible as plastic when it comes to joining wooden additions to them.

The main consideration in doing work on a wooden stock is to refinish it and keep its final appearance attractive in terms of grain and the overall lines. The type of wood you add to the stock isn't critical provided it is a hardwood; pine and other soft woods will not produce very good results.

Adding a higher comb for a better cheek weld is fairly easy to accomplish. After the buttplate has been removed, use a saw to cut off the top inch or so of the stock where the new cheek piece will be added. The square of new wood can then be glued onto the flat area created on the comb (cheek area) of the stock. While epoxy or cabinet-maker's glue will secure the new wooden cheek piece in place very tightly, it's also wise to drill holes in the stock and new comb and place dowel rods into them. This will greatly strengthen the new comb and make it considerably less likely to slip off if you accidentally drop the rifle.

Once the glue holding the new wood in place has had time to set up, you can start reshaping the cheekpiece. This shaping should first and foremost feel good to *your* face and allow you to view through the scope without craning your head to locate it. The appearance of your cheek rest is of secondary importance.

The height of the cheekpiece has more to do with your facial structure than anything else. But you can come close to the height you need by having the top of the new cheek rest even with the center of the Mini-14's bore.

When the shape is about right, use fine sandpaper, a fine rasp or file, and/or a draw knife to get the surface smooth and properly curved. For the most pleasing finish, it's wise to strip the old finish off the entire stock and refinish it so it has a uniform appearance.

The Mini-14 stock can also be reworked in several ways to improve its feel. A pistol-grip/skeletonized stock can be created by gluing wood onto some areas of the stock (using the technique above) while cutting parts out in other areas.

Those using the rifle for sporting or target shooting often enjoy the improved grip offered by checkering on the grip and foreguard areas of the stock. Checkering can be added fairly easily with some simple tools available from Brownells. (The NRA's *Gunsmithing Guide* and some of its other books go into the details of checkering stocks.)

Removing small amounts of wood from the stock can also be of help to some shooters. Those with small hands may see an improvement if the grip area is thinned. Cheek rests and the foregrip may also be altered, but care should be taken because it is easy to remove too much wood from these areas and ruin the stock.

Whether they have an out-of-the-box stock or one that's been highly customized, Mini-14s are often fired using only a scope for sighting. If you're planning on only using a scope on your rifle and will never use the iron sights, you should consider removing the sights from your rifle. This will make it lighter and can greatly improve its appearance as well. (Those who plan to use the rifle for combat or survival purposes will probably want to retain the iron sights for emergency use if the scope is damaged, however.)

To remove the sights, simply drift out the roll pin in the front sight base and then push the front sight out over the front of the barrel. The front sight base is pretty firmly attached to many rifles so you'll need to place a heavy drift punch against the rear surface of the front sight and use a mallet to slowly hammer it off. Be as gentle as possible when doing this, taking care not to damage the muzzle. Be forewarned that the drift punch will probably scar the front sight.

With the Ranch Rifle models of the Mini-14 and Mini-30, the rear sight can be removed easily as well by simply drifting it out one side of the notch cut into the receiver. This is also also possible with standard sights, but you have a bit more "stuff" to remove and the rear of the receiver will look a little odd after the sight is gone. The sight base can be removed from the top of the receiver with a grinder, but the end result isn't great. Your best bet is to purchase a Ranch Rifle in the first place if you wish to remove the rear sight for a cleaner look to your rifle. This will also simplify scope mounting.

Trigger pull can also affect the accuracy of the Mini-14 and is therefore a major consideration for many shooters. Fortunately, most Mini-14s not only come with good pulls from the factory, the action can be modified by a gunsmith easily. (And the Mini-14 lacks the creep and long travel of many "military-style rifles," making it most ideal when target shooting or varminting.) Modification of the trigger pull is a job best avoided by amateurs since it's easy to create a dangerous situation. However, there is one simple way to improve the feel of the trigger pull, and that is by "mating" the hammer and trigger.

The procedure consists of removing the trigger group, cocking back the hammer, and then pushing it forward very hard while the other hand pulls the trigger (taking care to restrain the hammer to keep it from banging against the front of the trigger housing). After doing this several times, you'll often discover that the pull is smoother and a bit lighter.

For those with the know-how, it's also possible to very lightly stone the surfaces of the trigger and hammer where they make contact. This must be done *very* carefully and just enough to polish the two surfaces without removing much metal or in any way altering the shape. Removing only a little too much metal can ruin either or both parts or make the gun very dangerous, so if you're not absolutely sure about what you're doing, leave this type of work to a skilled gunsmith.

Some shooters claim to be able to reduce the pull of the Mini-14 by allowing one of the legs of its spring to slip past its restraining position to rest lower than it normally would. Again, such a modification must be approached with caution and is better left to a gunsmith.

One modification skilled amateurs might wish to tackle is the installation of the Mini-14 Trigger Kit developed by Tom Provost and sold by his company, tAP. The assembly is installed easily by following the directions that come with the kit and will lower the pull to around 2 3/4 pounds, rather than the 4-pound pull of most rifles. No alteration of any of the original rifle's parts is required, nor are special tools.

Target shooters and varminters are generally unconcerned about how much energy a bullet has as long as it gets to the target properly. But there has always been a group of detractors who question whether the .223 is suitable for combat or hunting game. (For those who don't feel that the .223 is sufficient for such work, then the Mini-30's 7.62x39mm cartridge seems most ideal; it packs a punch nearly equal to the old .30-30 cartridge that has been tried and proven through the twentieth century.) However, it's a mistake to look at the .223 as an anemic cartridge, especially in its more modern loads.

While conventional wisdom has dictated that the .223 cartridge is "way too small for hunting deer," many hunters have used it as such. And while there are cases of deer running off as if they could care less about being hit by a .223 bullet (just as occurs from time to time with the powerful .308 and .30-06 cartridges), this doesn't seem to be the case too often. Medium-sized game taken at closer ranges with precisely placed shots invariably drop, often in their tracks. Hunters who have used the .223 on deer or antelope almost inevitably remark that the animal "dropped in its tracks" or "fell like it was pole-axed." This makes sense. After all, cartridges with similar power (like the .44 Magnum) or even considerably less power (like the .357 Magnum) have been exploited by handgunners for taking deer and other medium-size game for years.

The key in hunting is not power, but shot placement. It is poor shot placement that has allowed many game animals to flee after being struck by the most powerful of hunting bullets which—according to paper calculations—should have brought them down. (For those who'd like to take a look at just how important shot placement is, the article, "Of Power and Placement," by H.V. Stent that appears in the 1989 edition of *Gun Digest* will be of interest. The author relates many "impossible" kills of game animals, including three grizzly bears killed by one shot each with the diminutive .32 Special, a .25-35 Winchester rifle that was regularly utilized to take moose, and of .22 LR bullets being used for basically everything at close ranges. Finally, he recounts the story of a very successful guide and hunter who, with the puny .32-20 cartridge, took deer, black bear, cougar, and mountain goats over a forty-year stretch. The article doesn't make the logical step to looking at the capability of the .223, with its muzzle energy of 1,282 to 1,323 FPE, depending on the load and bullet. However, the .223 would have to be considered adequate for at least medium-sized game, provided the shooter has the skill to place the bullet correctly.)

That said, the type of bullet you use for hunting such animals is an important consideration. You don't want to employ varminting bullets when hunting medium-size game since these projectiles sometimes cause only superficial wounds that don't down the animal quickly. More substantial bullets are capable of causing fatal wounds to animals quickly by severing the spinal column or penetrating the heart or brain.

Remington, Federal, and Winchester all offer excellent expanding bullets suitable for hunting. The actual type can vary according to the shooter's tastes and thoughts. Some using the .223 prefer FMJ ammunition for hunting; others prefer an expanding bullet. And some seem to be having greater success with the heavy SS109-style bullet developed for NATO. (With the 7.62x39mm used in the Mini-30, the HP bullet generally gets the nod for hunting. Unlike the .223 bullet, which generally breaks apart, the FMJ in the 7.62x39mm chambering generally plows through an animal, doing minimal damage.)

Because bullet placement is important, you should purchase quality ammunition from a major manufacturer. Do not ever be tempted to use corrosive or even mildly corrosive ammunition manufactured overseas. While this ammunition is available at a lower price, it will quickly ruin a quality gun like the Mini-14 or Mini-30, even if you take care to clean it. Some of the corrosive residue is likely to remain behind in the gas system, gas port, or another hard-to-reach location. It's better to spend a few extra pennies per round and not trash your firearm.

Of course, the catch to hunting with a .223 rifle is the fact that some states have outlawed .22-caliber centerfire cartridges for taking deer and similar game. You might be able to get a Mini-14 rechambered for the 6mm/.223 Remington wildcat (also known as the 6x45mm) or a similar cartridge created by coupling the .223 Remington cartridge and a slightly larger bullet. But if you live in such an area, the easiest route is simply to purchase a Mini-30 and have at it with the more powerful cartridge. (Given the expense of having a Mini-14 reworked for a new cartridge, this is also probably more cost effective and gives the shooter two guns rather than one in the process.)

Small game hunting is a different story: both the .223 and 7.62x39mm cartridges are much too powerful. Shooting small game with either will leave a bloody bunch of feathers or fur where a bunny or bird once was. Fortunately, a .22 LR conversion kit is available for the Mini-14 and—as noted in later chapters—there are several .22 rifles that can be modified so their operation and sight picture are nearly identical to the Mini-14.

In addition to allowing you to realize some carry-over in habits from one gun to another, a .22 LR conversion kit or rifle that operates like your Mini-14 can save quite a bit of money if you practice much. Each bang of the .22 LR instead of a .223 saves around a quarter or more (at the time of this writing). That means if you'd normally go out and fire several hundred rounds in a practice session, using the .22 LR kit or .22 rifle rather than the Mini-14 would save you enough to pay for the conversion kit or rifle in just seven or eight shooting sessions.

Currently, Jonathan Arthur Ciener's Hohrein .22 LR adapter for the Mini-14 is *the* adapter kit. It's well made and functions reliably. It comes with a 30-round magazine and sells for about $119. Converting the Mini-14 from .223 to .22 LR or back to its original chambering takes only a few moments and doesn't call for any special tools. (One note: this kit does *not* work on the 180 series Mini-14s.)

When hunting, plinking, or target shooting with the .22

LR, you'll discover you have a wide array of ammunition available to you. Always be sure to tailor the ammunition to the shooting you're doing. If you're shooting at longer ranges (perhaps at the mini iron targets that are becoming popular with many .22 LR shooters), then CCI's Mini-Mag LR HS, Federal's Hi-Power, or Winchester's 37-grain HP are good—with Winchester's Silhouette ammunition (a 42-grain lead bullet) giving fantastic results clear out to 100 or even 125 yards.

If you need extra accuracy for target or hunting work, Winchester's R1 Match or Federal's Champion Target ammunition work well. However, those using a conversion kit should bear in mind that the accuracy of these cartridges won't be fully realized with a .22 conversion kit. This is because the .223 cartridge is slightly different in diameter from a standard .22 LR bullet; the fast twist of the new Mini-14s also isn't conducive to great accuracy. Therefore, it's better to purchase a .22 rifle similar to the Mini-14 if you need optimal accuracy.

"Hypervelocity" rounds like the CCI Stinger, Federal HP Spitfire, Winchester SuperMax, and Remington Viper mark the upper limits of the .22 LR cartridges in regard to potential wounding capability. These little zingers have nearly as much power as most .32 ACP cartridges and actually give better results than most FMJ .32 bullets when hitting flesh-and-blood targets. This makes them ideal for some types of pest control and varminting. (If you wish to take small game, however, the solid point .22 LR bullet coupled with careful bullet placement is generally the best bet since less meat will be destroyed.)

Finally, mention must be made of the .22 LR's little cousin, the .22 CB Cap. Originally created in the 1800s as a low-velocity round for shooting galleries, this cartridge has made a comeback in recent years. Its most recent reincarnation utilizes the brass casing designed for the .22 Long Rifle.

This makes it practical to fire the cartridge in the Mini-14 with a conversion kit, or in a .22 rifle.

The .22 CB Cap produces a minimal report so it's ideal for indoor practice (with thick phone books, scrap wood, or other material for a backstop) or for training beginners without having to worry about excessive recoil or noise. The .22 CB Long doesn't have enough energy to cycle a semiauto action, so it has to be hand-cycled between shots. But this can be a plus since the gun's action doesn't clatter if you're trying to snipe on game without giving yourself away, and it also turns the firearm into a single-shot trainer for beginners. CCI, Federal, and Remington all offer nearly identical .22 CB Cap cartridges.

While there are no Mini-14s chambered for centerfire pistol cartridges, there are several carbines that are similar to the Mini-14 in operation (more on these later). These firearms offer a step up in power from the .22 LR and, in effect, bridge the gap between the .223 and .22 LR. While handgun cartridges are not as ideal for urban/indoor combat needs as they once were, thanks to Federal's Blitz cartridge, they still hold potential as a hunting round.

For hunting small game on the larger end of the scale (which covers quite a variety of game) as well as for self-defense, Winchester Silvertips, Federal's HP and Nyclad, and CCI's Lawman JHP and Blazer JHP are first choices. These cartridges offer reliable expansion for maximum energy transfer and are actually designed for law enforcement and self-defense.

For hunting smaller game with the 9mm cartridge, you need less energy transfer to the target so there's a minimum of meat damage. In such a case, FMJ bullets will be more ideal. Fortunately, most of the target/practice cartridges offered by PMC, Federal, Winchester, Samson, Remington, and CCI all come topped with FMJ bullets.

Mention should also be made of the .45 ACP since the

Marlin Camp Rifle, which will be covered in a later chapter, is also chambered for this popular pistol cartridge. Once believed to be the top dog of handgun cartridges, the .45 ACP isn't as powerful as was earlier thought. But it isn't an anemic little pip-squeak, either; it holds its own pretty well with the 9mm Luger. The catch with the .45 ACP is that it's big and heavy, so not nearly as many .45 rounds can be carried in a same-size magazine when compared to cartridges like the 9mm.

This isn't much of a consideration, however, since most "gun fights" are concluded with just one or two shots. So even the limited capacity of most .45 ACP firearms gives room to spare. It's just that an occasional gun battle does go beyond a few shots, and that causes many people to switch to higher capacity 9mm firearms.

For those electing to use the .45 ACP for self-defense or hunting, the CCI 200-grain HP bullet is top dog in terms of one-shot fight stopping; Winchester's 185-grain STHP, Federal's 185-grain HP, and Remington's 185-grain HP are close runners-up.

For target shooters, Federal's 230-grain FMJ-Match and 185-grain FMJ-SWC Match, Samson's FMJ 230 Match, CCI-Blazer's TMJ Match (available both in 185- and 200-grain loadings), Hornady's 200-grain C/T Match, and Remington's 185-grain Match TMWC are all capable of excellent results. If you're looking for the best accuracy you can get, try several different brands of ammunition in an auto to determine which works best, since it can vary from one firearm to the next.

Regardless of the type of rifle or what you use it for, you'll have to clean it carefully and protect the muzzle end of the gun if you are to maintain its accuracy. Be sure to follow the recommended procedures for cleaning the firearm and take care not to damage the bore—especially toward the crown—through improper cleaning techniques.

CHAPTER 4

SAW Versions of the Mini-14 and Mini-30

It's possible to create a high-firepower super-system rifle built around a Mini-14 or, to some extent, the Mini-30, and it can be done with very little effort by utilizing several off-the-shelf accessories. But before you jump into such modifications, it's prudent to consider the thinking behind the development of such weapons so you can learn from others' successes and mistakes.

Modern combat tactics are often based on firepower. No one (except for TV freaks, perhaps) will argue that firepower is all that's needed to win battles. But it certainly helps. And even a skilled marksman will become a more dangerous adversary when the firepower of the weapon he carries has been boosted.

Since the first Gatling guns were introduced in combat, military personnel and civilians who've had to defend themselves have appreciated the edge greater firepower can give them. It's no accident that the development of repeating firearms coincided with the abrupt decline in the American West of roving bands of outlaws and Indians in the 1800s.

It wasn't until World War I that *mobile* firepower that could be brought to bear in very heavy fire was realized with the introduction of the Lewis gun. Until that time, repeating guns fired quickly only for limited periods before reloading was necessary, and machine guns, which were heavy and awkward to move and operate, were treated like artillery field pieces.

For all practical purposes, the Lewis gun was what we today would call an LMG (light machine gun) or SAW (squad automatic weapon), since it could be toted by one man and used the same cartridges carried by members of the rifle squad it traveled with. The Lewis gun quickly established a reputation for being deadly in combat; troops dubbed it the "Military Mower." The Lewis gun was not as robust as one might hope for, but it proved that a lightweight, high-firepower package was an important asset in combat—a fact that continues to influence military design and tactics. (For a detailed look at the Lewis gun, refer to J. David Truby's book, *The Lewis Gun*, available from Paladin Press.)

The effectiveness of the Lewis gun is the principal reason most modern military squads carry an SAW or LMG with them. But as the size of the cartridge in the rifles carried by ground troops has shrunk, a debate has raged as to what cartridge the SAW and LMG should be chambered for.

For a time, many military thinkers argued that the .223 cartridge was not powerful enough for SAW or LMG use, and in many ways they were right. But that has changed with the introduction of the new NATO version of the SS109 developed by Fabrique Nationale. The bullet from this round actually out-penetrates the .308 Winchester/7.62mm NATO when fired at steel helmets or mild steel plates. And Olin/Winchester recently introduced their Penetrator version of the .223, which actually outperforms the SS109 in terms of penetration. With these cartridges capable of inflicting deadly wounds with some accuracy to eight hundred or even a thousand yards, it isn't hard to see why the armed forces of the world are chambering their SAWs for them.

The performance of these new .223 cartridges is the reason heavy-barreled versions of assault rifles and small machine guns like the FN Minimi; Steyr AUG H-BAR; Colt CMG-2 and H-BAR; Germany's HK-23 E, HK-73, and HK-GR6; Enfield LSW; Beretta M70-78; Singapore's Ultimax 100; and the Spanish Ameli, among others, compete for jobs that were traditionally handled by .308 or .30-06 LMGs in the past.

So if you decide to create a do-it-yourself SAW around the Mini-14, you'll be building on the current trend toward the use of such firearms by modern military forces. (If you're of the old school of thought that would like a bit more punch in an SAW, you can build your system around the Mini-30. While most of the modifications and accessories described below are aimed at the Mini-14, many can be easily adapted to the more powerful Mini-30.) Whether you go with the Mini-14 or a more powerful Mini-30-based SAW system, there are two features found on most military SAWs that you'll likely not be able to duplicate.

One is the quick-change barrel. The other is the belt-feed mechanism. While many modern SAWs are lacking one or both of these devices, that doesn't seem to hinder their overall effectiveness and may even enhance them in some environments.

In fact, many European and Asian armies are currently fielding heavy-barrel versions of their assault rifles as SAWs without any provision of a quick-change barrel. Even the U.S. Army, after requiring that the FN Minimi be created with a quick-change barrel, has been fielding the guns *without* the spare barrels. In such cases, the machine gunner is simply expected to exercise discipline so as not to melt his barrel with excessive shooting. (Given the weight of the Minimi—14 1/2 pounds empty—a Mini-14 owner can actually carry a spare rifle and end up with a package that weighs about the same as the FN machine gun with just a spare barrel!)

Likewise, the belt-feed option on SAWs is a dubious asset given the dirt and chaos of most modern battlefields. With World War I-vintage rifles having only an 8-round magazine, a belt-fed machine gun had obvious advantages. But with 40- and 90-round magazines now readily available for the Mini-14 and other rifles, and the availability of connectors capable of joining magazines together, the belt mechanism doesn't seem so important. So if you're contemplating designing a Mini-14 SAW, you shouldn't be deterred by the lack of belt feed or a quick-change barrel.

What about selective fire? Undoubtedly a few readers will have a selective-fire version of the Mini-14 or be in a government agency that can still legally modify a Mini-14 to such a configuration. But for the rest of us, it seems doubtful that all that much is lost through being limited to semiauto fire. After all, automatic fire wastes a lot of ammunition and, given the high cyclic rate of most machine guns, doesn't do much to improve a shooter's chances of prevailing in combat. Given the fact that the .223 cartridge is effective on human targets, one has to wonder what advantage is really gained by scoring a number of hits on an enemy.

Conversely, if you miss when firing in the automatic mode, you miss with a number of rounds rather than one. So while a selective-fire Mini-14 might have psychological advantages, its actual advantage isn't as great as one might imagine, especially given the fact that a skilled shooter can work the trigger of a semiauto at speeds that approach those of automatic weapons.

Large-capacity magazines are a necessity for the SAW. Fortunately, extended box magazines for the Mini-14 with

40-round Federal Ordnance magazines (in blued metal or nickel finish) are readily available from L.L. Baston for $33 each.

For those creating an SAW around the Mini-30, L.L. Baston also offers U.S.-made, steel, 30-round magazines for $48 and a long 50-round magazine for $85, as well as a plastic 15-round magazine for $25.

Also available for the Mini-14 is Eagle's Beta-Mag 14-35, which is made of smoked plastic and holds thirty-five rounds. This transparent magazine allows you to see at a glance how much ammunition is in it—a definite advantage over metal magazines. Oddly enough, these magazines are only half an inch longer than standard 30-round metal magazines, thanks to a pair of spiral springs inside them. Eagle also offers a high-capacity magazine for the Mini-30; the transparent polymer magazine holds eighteen cartridges. Both of these magazines retail for $16 apiece.

High-capacity magazines can be joined in several ways to increase the amount of ammunition that is carried with the rifle. A second magazine can be an asset because it reduces the time needed for reloading.

Two of Eagle's Beta-Mag 14-35 magazines. Useful for creating an SAW system, these magazines are made of smoked plastic and hold thirty-five rounds each. These magazines are only half an inch longer than a standard 30-round metal magazine. (Photo courtesy of Eagle Manufacturing.)

One way *not* to connect magazines is to tape them together so one points down and the other up. The one pointing down is apt to have its lips damaged or get full of dirt if you bump or drop it. A better way of connecting two magazines is with the Mag-Pac, also available from L.L. Baston, or with Choate Machine & Tool's Magazine Clip Connectors. Both fit snugly on a pair of magazines, creating the proper space between them so that they can be carried with one in the well of an AR-15 while the other sits alongside it.

This keeps the spare magazine up out of the dirt if prone shooting is required, but allows magazines to be exchanged quickly by depressing the magazine release and then chugging the new magazine into place. The Mag-Pac costs $15 and Choate's Magazine Clip Connectors (which are a bit more compact but need a screwdriver to mount or remove from the magazines) are $16 each.

For many armies that have elected to use magazines rather than belt-feeds on their SAWs, the drum magazine is coupled to the firearm. These large magazines are often available to civilian and police shooters as well.

Drum magazines have earned a poor reputation. The reason for this is partly justified since many older designs were plagued with jams. Many of these older magazines used a wind-up clock arrangement with a coiled spring inside the drum, which worked haphazardly at best. Those used in the Thompson submachine gun and similar weapons were notorious for their tendency to jam. More recently, during the 1970s, a plastic version of the snail or drum magazine was marketed in the United States that soured a new generation of shooters due to its tendency to jam.

With modern technology and designs, the drum magazine seems to be finally overcoming the problems, however. The Chinese RPK magazine seems to work fairly well, as does the drum magazine designed for the Ultimax.

One good drum magazine recently available for the Mini-14 is MWG's 90-Round Drum, currently available from L.L. Baston for $60. The 90-round magazine's body takes advantage of modern plastics, so it's light and rustproof. An additional advantage of the plastic is that the magazine's back panel is clear so you can determine how much ammunition is left in it with a glance. The 90-round magazine curves to the left (unlike most earlier and current designs, which ride directly under the magazine well). This makes it shorter than a 30-round magazine, which can be important during prone shooting. Internally, the unit uses a coil spring in a widely spaced, snail-shaped column to propel cartridges through the magazine with considerably less chance of a jam.

It's interesting to note that Colt Firearms has recently started offering the 90-Round Drum to military buyers with their LMG version of the M16 H-BAR. Given the military user's need for reliability and ease of maintenance, this would seem to indicate that Colt feels the 90-round magazine is reliable enough for combat and a notable asset to their LMG/H-BAR's capability.

There are minor shortcomings to the 90-round magazine. The plastic will break if it's really abused, though a blow that would break it would undoubtedly ruin a metal magazine as well, so the tradeoff in materials seems justified.

Trying to cram too many rounds into the mechanism will cause feeding problems and, of course, loading ninety rounds into a magazine isn't quick. But the 90-round magazine comes with a special cartridge-pushing tool and a charger that make the task a little easier, especially on the last thirty rounds loaded into the magazine, since the spring gets pretty "pushy" at that point. (Some shooters feel that the spring in the 90-Round Drum fatigues if the magazine is left loaded for extended periods. While this seems doubtful given a spring's ability to stay compressed for decades without losing its tem-

The 90-Round Drum rides a little closer to the stock than a 30-round magazine, while providing three times as much firepower. The magazine's clear plastic back shows at a glance if it's nearly empty.

per and flexibility, shooters may choose to avoid storing fully loaded 90-Round Drums.)

All of these problems are minor, however. If a little care is taken, the 90-round magazine works well and offers a lot of firepower in a tight package that works well with the Mini-14.

For those who, for one reason or another, can't own a selective-fire version of the Mini-14, U.S. inventors seem to have come to the rescue in one way or another. While it would seem that weapons that allow a firearm to shoot bursts of fire would be illegal, they in fact fall into the loopholes of the law by not changing the action of the Mini-14's trigger, which still only fires one shot each time it is pulled in true semiautomatic fashion.

The B.M.F. Activator was one of the first such devices. It's currently available for $20 from L.L. Baston. The B.M.F. Activator's Gatling gun-like crank fastens to the trigger

guard of a Mini-14 (or most other rifles) so cranking it causes a cam to cycle. As this cam moves back and forth, it trips
the Mini-14's trigger and causes it to fire. Thus, turning the
crank moves the cam in and out and bursts are fired from the
rifle. The big shortcoming of the B.M.F. activator is that its
plastic body warps if it's left on a Mini-14 for any length of
time.

A similar mechanism is the Ultimate from Firearm
Systems and Design. This unit, sold for $130, acts like a pis-
tol grip when mounted on a standard Mini-14 stock. A long
lever on the unit is pulled and pushed by the shooter's fingers, causing the trigger to be tripped by a small cam in the
mechanism when it is pulled and then again by a second
cam when the lever is pushed. In effect, this gives two shots
rather than one for each cycle of the lever. By cycling the
lever quickly, you can fire short bursts from the rifle.

The third burst-fire mechanism available is the Tri-Burst,
from Orpheus Industries, for $40. The Tri-Burst clamps onto
the trigger guard of a Mini-14 so a ring hangs under the
guard. The shooter's trigger finger goes into this levered ring;
pulling it back creates three pushes against the trigger of the
Mini-14 for a 3-round burst.

It's doubtful that any of these three units would be of
much real use in an actual combat situation. They are awkward, and it's easy to accidentally fire them if you walk
around with a round chambered in your Mini-14 and the
unit ready to go. But all three are a lot of fun and give a
shooter the chance to gain the feel of automatic fire and see
what it can—and can't—do.

Regardless of whether high rates of fire are being created
with true auto fire, a burst-fire gadget, or simply by fast finger action on a standard semiauto, the Mini-14's barrel can
overheat with extended shooting. In extreme cases, this
overheating can actually damage the barrel if firing continues and can create the hazard of "cook-offs" (rounds that

ignite and fire without being struck by the firing pin due to the heat transferred through the brass after the cartridge sits in the hot chamber of the barrel).

The best way to prevent barrel overheating is what the military calls "fire discipline." You simply don't fire excessively and stay out of combat situations where you get cornered or ambushed and are forced to shoot excessively in order to escape. (That's easier said than done, and often there will be a decided psychological advantage in being able to shoot prodigious amounts of ammunition.)

So how can you reduce the problem of barrel overheating or at least make it so it takes longer to become a problem?

One way is to increase the air flow over the hot barrel. If your Mini-14 has a solid wooden handguard (as the early models do), then you need to purchase a ventilated handguard, available from a number of companies (Ram-Line offers an excellent one for $15). These can be snapped into place, and they allow air to circulate around the barrel.

Some do-it-yourselfers will want to increase the number

A ventilated handguard will help prevent heat buildup from the Mini-14 barrel. Adding vents farther back will speed the cooling of the barrel, but it also increases the danger of debris fouling the operating lever.

or size of ventilation holes in the handguard. This is easily done with a drill and file. Just bear in mind that the solid handguard also keeps dirt out of the Mini-14 mechanism. Be sure you don't trade one problem for another.

Heat buildup can also be handled with a heavier barrel since the extra metal will act as a heat sink. If you wish to go to the extra expense, getting a heavy varminter barrel will increase the number of shots that can be put through your Mini-14 before you experience overheating.

Fluted barrels also offer a way of reducing heat buildup. A fluted barrel radiates heat faster since it has greater surface area; this enables it to cool off more quickly. A fluted barrel still heats up faster than a heavier barrel, but not as fast as a smaller barrel, and it cools off faster than either.

One problem with a fluted barrel is its expense. The fluting has to be done virtually by hand on a milling machine. This labor is expensive. But if you're really interested in overcoming heat buildup, then you may want to consider having a gunsmith flute a varminter barrel for you in order to reduce your Mini-14's weight and increase the speed with which it cools off after being fired excessively. (One nice thing about a fluted barrel is that it will be nearly as stiff as a heavy barrel; this means it will retain the accuracy it had before fluting while weighing considerably less.)

In theory, it would seem that a heat sink in the form of an aluminum sleeve with heavy fluting might be added to the Mini-14's barrel, possibly ahead of the handguard and gas block. But such heat-transfer techniques haven't been experimented with to any great extent. The Lewis gun apparently had such a device designed for it, and it wasn't too effective. Consequently, this might well be a technological dead end that looks good in print but is poor in practice.

Because lightweight rifles have a tendency to "dance" as recoil throws them about during rapid fire, a method of anchoring the gun is often desirable. In the past, the gun was simply anchored by its weight; this works well but is tough on the gunner who's burdened with the weapon in the field.

The muzzle brake and compensator are more modern solutions that don't require excessive weight. These counterbalance the recoil forces with a jet of gases leaving the barrel so that the Mini-14 remains more or less stationary with a reduced recoil pushing the gun straight back. The idea of taming the recoil by diverting gas is far from ideal. But until recently, such devices were only effective on large cannons and not on small arms. That has changed.

One effective, but crude, compensator is the simple deflector that can be found on many AK-47 rifles. Such a device is simply a tube that's chopped off at an angle so gas is shunted upward slightly when the gun is fired. This gas jet shoves the muzzle of the gun downward. Such a muzzle compensator can be created by simply cutting the muzzle of the Mini-14 off at a right angle with the more open half of the barrel pointing upward. The catch is that such deflectors are noisy, create a lot of muzzle flash, and don't promote accuracy of the barrel.

Another type of Soviet muzzle compensator that is seen in the United States is the AK-74-style brake (which was, in fact, modeled after modern cannon muzzle brakes). In addition to reducing the upward deflection of the muzzle, the AK-74-style attachment also acts as a muzzle brake to decrease felt recoil. It works well but still does little to hide flash and creates a noisy blast of gas that can also kick up clouds of dust in prone shooting. These brakes (designed for the AR-15 rifle) can be purchased from Rhino Replacement Parts for $40. The Mini-14 barrel should then be threaded by a gunsmith and the brake screwed to it.

If you're going to the trouble of getting the muzzle of your Mini-14 threaded, however, you might as well get an even better muzzle brake. Fortunately, the United States hasn't been sitting on the sidelines in muzzle compensator development, so there are some other muzzle brakes to consider.

Perhaps one of the simpler solutions has been created on the standard M16/AR-15-A2 flash hider. This is the standard "bird cage" design, which does very well at hiding muzzle flash with its bottom vents closed. This causes gas to jet upward through the open vents and thereby push the muzzle downward. Not only is this design effective in cutting down muzzle flash, it doesn't raise dust during prone shooting and it isn't noisy. About the only area where it falls behind the AK-74 design is in recoil reduction—but that isn't much of a consideration with the .223.

For those who don't wish to go through the hassle of having the barrel of the Mini-14 threaded to accept an AR-15 flash hider, several companies offer similar bird-cage flash hiders with the lower side unslotted. These are designed to be slipped onto the barrel of the Mini-14 and are held in

Choate Machine & Tool's slip-on flash hider is easy to mount. The front sight's drift pin is removed, the flash hider slipped on, and a longer pin added to hold the hider in place. The lack of vents on the bottom forces the barrel downward to help counter muzzle rise.

place with a roll pin or hex screw. (Those fastened by hex screws should be carefully checked for tightness, and Loctite or a similar glue should be used on the screw to keep it from shaking loose.)

Choate Machine & Tool has slip-on hiders that simply go around the front sight of the Mini-14 (where they're held by a replacement roll pin) available in blued and stainless fin-

Choate's replacement front sight/flash hiders for the Mini-14. *Top*: The long, M14-style hider, which is very effective in reducing flash. *Bottom left*: The stainless version of the M16-style bird-cage hider. *Bottom right*: the blued version.

ishes for $25. Ram-Line offers a similar slip-on flash hider for the Mini-14 for $20 in the blued version and $35 in stainless steel.

Choate's replacement front sight/flash hider is similar to that of the M14 rifle (with two "dog ears" to help with leading moving targets). This is a bit harder to mount, but many people prefer its looks and sight picture to that of the Mini-14 front sight. Cost is $30 for blued or $33 for stainless steel. Choate also offers a similar M14-style flash hider that's longer but also does a better job of eliminating muzzle flash;

Eagle's front sight/ flash hider for the Mini-14 has the sight post surrounded by a circular ring, similar to that of the Heckler & Koch G3/HK-91 rifle series. (Photo courtesy of Eagle Manufacturing.)

prices are the same—$30 for blued and $33 for stainless.

Eagle offers a front sight/flash hider for $36 in stainless or blued versions. Its sight post is surrounded by a circular ring, similar to that of the Heckler & Koch G3/HK-91 rifle series. The lower vents are further down on the Eagle flash hider, making it less effective in recoil reduction, though some may still prefer it due to its H&K-style sight picture.

One system that is effective in reducing recoil, while still doing well at reducing muzzle flash and not raising dust or being noisy, is the Fabian Muzzle Stabilizer distributed by Fabian Brothers. This compensator has a number of carefully placed holes that jet gas upward and to one side so the shooter can compensate for both the upward and sideways movement of the rifle. In addition to acting as a compensator, the unit acts as a muzzle brake to reduce felt recoil by around 40 percent and also reduces flash. In a world of compromise, the Fabian system is a very good solution to a number of problems. Cost is $35.

Another solution to controlling the Mini-14/SAW during firing is to mount a forward pistol grip under the handguard. This allows the shooter to have a firmer hold on an automatic weapon during sustained firing.

Such grips are seen on older firearms like the Thompson and Hyde submachine guns and on up to the new versions of the M60 and Colt's newest military M16 H-BAR and LMG. Forward grips work with varying success but might be considered by those needing a bit more control of a Mini-14/SAW. If you opt for such a device, it's simple to fasten it onto the Mini-14, especially on those models that have a plastic stock.

The easiest of these to mount is from E&L Manufacturing. It consists of a rounded, H&K-style forward grip that fastens onto the ventilated barrel shroud that comes with it. The catch to this arrangement is that it requires removal of the front sight to mount it. It also places the

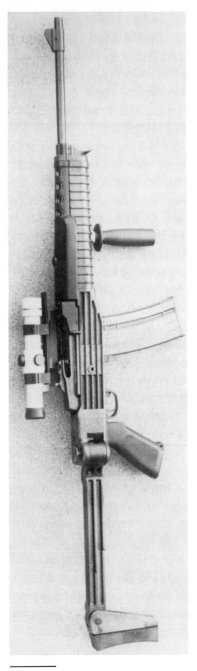

front grip very far forward of the stock. Cost is $30.

A better arrangement is to purchase an AR-15 pistol grip and fasten it to the underside of the Mini-14 stock. This is a little tricky: the stock is thin on this part of the rifle and care must be taken not to interfere with the operation of the gas piston or damage the forearm liner inside the stock.

Unfortunately, many shooters will find that the AR-15-style grip, while great for the shooting hand, isn't too ideal for the off hand due to the angle the arm takes in clearing the extended magazine that most Mini-14s carry. The solution to this is to adopt the Heckler & Koch MP5K forward grip. This grip has a

An H&K-style forward grip (originally sold by E&L Manufacturing for attaching to a barrel shroud) is mounted under the handguard of this Ram-Line stock to help steady the Mini-14. Aimpoint's 2000L scope is mounted on an Eagle QD base. The flash hider has been left off to keep the gun compact when the stock is folded.

round, peglike shape that's easily created from aluminum or wood (especially if turned on a wood or metal lathe). Mounting an H&K-style grip is the same as for the previous grip, though there's less of a problem since it has no front or back to it.

The current "Rolls Royce" of forward grips is Tom Provost's The Handle, offered by tAP for $35. It's easy to screw into the stock and is readily adjustable so the user can rotate it back and forth under the stock to create the grip angle that suits his needs. This allows the Mini-14 to be carried with the handle sticking out from the side for assault attack when shooting on the move, or quickly rotated straight down under the stock when firing from the prone position. At the time of this writing, work is being done to incorporate a bipod into the inside of The Handle so it can be pulled out quickly for prone shooting. A choice of aluminum or black plastic is available.

Tom Provost's The Handle is screwed onto a Mini-14 stock easily. It is readily adjustable so the user can rotate it back and forth under the stock to create the grip angle that suits his needs before tightening it into place. (Photo courtesy of tAP.)

Even if you don't go with The Handle or other forward grip device, you may want to use a bipod to steady your Mini-14, a la SAW. In the past, bipods on SAWs were chunky and heavy in order to help anchor the gun during firing. But since the muzzle brake makes such weight unnecessary (and even undesirable), those wanting a bipod will generally be most happy with a lightweight design.

A Mini-14 transformed to SAW configuration with Aimpoint scope, Ram-Line folder, Eagle scope mount, and 35-round magazine. The forward grip was added by screw-mounting a Ram-Line AR-15 grip onto the stock. A Ram-Line bipod and 90-Round Drum complete the system.

The Ram-Line bipod is extremely lightweight and is made almost entirely of plastic. The bipod can be taken off or placed on the rifle quickly and can be carried in a long pocket or pouch if it isn't needed.

The lightest and handiest bipod available on the commercial market is Ram-Line's plastic bipod. It uses the traditional clothespin-style first seen on the U.S. M16 rifle. Unlike the military version, however, the Ram-Line bipod is mostly plastic so it resists damage and rust. This handy $15 bipod snaps on and off a Mini-14 barrel in seconds and can be carried in a deep pocket or pouch when it isn't being used. The Ram-Line bipod can be modified somewhat so it's less apt to be knocked off the rifle. This would be a consideration if the Mini-14 were to be used for self-defense or carried in brush.

The simplest modification is to run a metal band over the top of the bipod and secure it to one of the sides below the jaws with two metal screws. This is easy work and only involves cutting some scrap metal to size and drilling two pilot holes in the metal and bipod. Metal screws are ideal; black spray paint will enable you to obtain a professional look. If care is used in making this modification, it will still be possible to remove the bipod from the rifle's barrel but nearly impossible to knock it off accidentally.

Another bipod that might be employed on your Mini-14/SAW is the Harris bipod (from Harris Engineering for $44.50). This unit can be attached to the front of a standard Mini-14 stock using a small adapter sold by Harris. The aluminum bipod can be folded or deployed very quickly and comes in two styles.

The standard Harris bipod is the 1A-LR. Another, the 1A-HR, has extra long legs that allow you to shoot from a sitting position. Unfortunately, the play in the 1A-HR makes it good only for single shots. The gun will start to travel with fast semiauto or automatic fire. This makes the 1A-LR more suitable to SAW designs. The old Harris bipod had spring-loaded legs that created some noise when unfolded. The new style requires the user to pull each leg out. This makes it a bit slower to deploy but also makes it

Stainless version of the Cherokee Featherweight bipod mounted on a Mini-14 Ranch Rifle with a Ruger-made folder. The bipod is very light and easy to deploy. It is mounted on the rifle stock with two screws.

quiet when the legs are extended.

Another fine bipod is the Cherokee Featherweight that, as its name suggests, weighs in at only 5.7 ounces. The bipod is made of steel and epoxy/fiberglass so it's strong enough to take a lot of abuse. Its legs fold under the rifle when not in use and can be deployed quickly and noiselessly with one hand. The standard black version of the Featherweight is $65; a stainless-steel version is $100.

Bipods are often mounted toward the front of the barrel to help reduce recoil. However, with a light bipod and a well-designed muzzle brake, it isn't necessary to place the bipod toward the muzzle. It can be placed further back. And the further back you have it toward the receiver, the quicker the SAW can be rotated on the axis of the bipod to engage targets. (In fact, you may discover that mounting a Cherokee or Harris bipod backward so it is just ahead of the receiver/magazine will be the ideal position.)

If a bipod is being used for prone firing, a stock with a hook on its underside near the buttpad may be an asset. This can be gripped by the off hand to push the stock against the shoulder. Sometimes these devices can be improvised with

an oversized rear-sling swivel; Choate's fixed Mini-14 pistol-grip stock has an E2 hook molded into it; simply buying it is the quickest route to take to obtain this feature.

Another accessory which is easily improvised is the shoulder rest that folds up from the buttplate. It sticks out from the rear of the butt and goes over the top of the shoulder to help keep the SAW in place when firing in the prone position.

These aren't the only way to steady an SAW during firing. The rifle can also be rested on the edge of branches, vehicles, or other objects. For best results, the hard objects should be padded with rags, a hat, or other improvised padding.

An extended magazine can also form a support, or monopod, for the rifle. Toward the end of World War II, the Germans often used the long magazines on their assault rifles this way. This same technique can be used with the Mini-14 holding a 30- or 40-round maga-

The E2 hook molded to the Choate fixed stock for the Mini-14 allows the shooter to use his off hand to keep the rifle in place when firing from the prone position. (Photo courtesy of Choate Machine & Tool.)

zine. This also does away with the catch-in-the-brush legs of a deployed bipod, and it decreases the weight of the SAW to boot. To protect the lower part of the magazine, it's wise to wrap padding or other protective material around its base. Before going to a lot of trouble and expense to obtain a bipod, you should at least try using an extended magazine to see if the monopod is suitable for your needs.

Since a Mini-14 SAW will probably be carried more than it's fired or placed in a permanent position, you will want to keep your creation as light as possible using the various techniques outlined in previous chapters. The weight of the Mini-14 can also be distributed with a wide sling to reduce its perceived burden. A padded hunting sling like those offered by Uncle Mike's (or perhaps a used M60 sling), modified for the assault carry, will also make the Mini-14 easier to carry for long periods of time.

For those needing a short package (perhaps for firing

A compact SAW created around a stainless Mini-14 with a Muzzlelite stock. The scope is an Aimpoint 2000L; the Choate flash hider helps control recoil. Rounding out the system are a 90-Round Drum from L.L. Baston and Ram-Line's plastic bipod.

Bipod-mounted bullpups can be of help with an SAW when shooting from certain positions.

from a vehicle, aboard a ship, or from cramped indoor areas), then the bullpup configuration would be ideal for the Mini-14 SAW. In such a case, the Muzzlelite stock covered earlier would be first choice for this conversion.

Of course, it would also be possible to create quasi-LMG versions of the Mini-14 SAW. Given the longer range and power of the 5.56mm NATO (SS-109) and Winchester Penetrator ammunition, it seems that this ammunition, coupled with the Mini-14's 1-in-7 twist and possibly selective-fire capabilities, would be capable of fulfilling some LMG roles.

Mounting a Mini-14 in the SAW configuration on a tripod would certainly give it many of the abilities of an LMG, including the capability to be fixed on an area or cover distant targets with grazing or plunging fire. And it could be adapted to a heavy military surplus tripod or vehicle mount, both of which are available as military surplus from companies like SARCO and Gun Parts Corporation.

But such super-heavy tripods and other mounts defeat the

pluses of the lightweight Mini-14 in many ways. A much lighter version of the standard military tripod would offer more mobility. Therefore, a do-it-yourselfer with design/welding skills would be better advised to create a lightweight tripod or pedestal mount of his own design for his Mini-14 LMG.

In order to increase their firepower, small-caliber

While more assault rifle than SAW, this rifle might perform many of the tasks normally handled by an SAW. Compared to most military SAWs, this is a lightweight, compact package. This gun has a Choate slip-on flash hider and an Eagle 35-round magazine.

machine guns have often been mounted side by side. (One of the best-known current examples of this system is the German antiaircraft mount for the MG3 LMG, which places two of these machine guns side by side at shoulder height, with the gunner having one on each of his shoulders while his hand operates each trigger.)

A pair of Mini-14s can be mounted in a similar manner, possibly overcoming some of the inadequacies that the .223 round might have in the LMG role in the process. Several inches must separate the two rifles to allow for ejection of the brass from the left rifle, as well as to allow its charging lever to be retracted and the chamber checked if necessary. Since brass from the left Mini-14 will bounce off the gun to its right and may strike the shooter in the process, an E&L brass catcher could be mounted on the left rifle (or both of them) to minimize this problem.

Ideally, the rifles will be on a tripod or other mount since the paired rifles will otherwise be quite awkward. Perhaps the best arrangement would be to have them mounted so one would be on each of the shooter's shoulders. Then each hand could grasp a pistol grip and control the trigger. In such an arrangement, both guns must be securely anchored and aligned so their point of aim is as near to the same point as possible.

Another dual system is outlined in the next chapter. It places a second gun beside or under the barrel of a Mini-14. This system would also enable two firearms to be fired by one operator, and it could be used to couple the Mini-14 under the barrel of an AR-15 or other firearm. Adding to the pluses of such a system using the AR-15 and Mini-14 is Ram-Line's 30-round magazine ($17), which fits and operates in either rifle. When these magazines are coupled together in pairs, they give a lot of firepower in interchangeable magazines that will fit in either the Mini-14 or AR-15 half of such a hybrid firearm.

Since the Mini-14 in any of the SAW or LMG configurations outlined in this chapter can burn up prodigious amounts of ammunition during practice, it's wise to find a source of inexpensive ammunition. Currently, PMC imports noncorrosive ammunition that bears a low price tag, and generic .223 ammunition is manufactured by Federal (American Eagle brand) and Winchester (USA). Offered by all three companies at very reasonable prices, military-type ammunition is ideal for safe, inexpensive practice sessions.

CHAPTER 5

Combination Guns Based on the Mini-14

Rifles and shotguns with double or even triple barrels are nothing new. The oldest muzzle loaders were such weapons. They were created to make firearms more flexible, firing a number of different calibers, and to increase their firepower. More recently, multibarreled weapons have been created in an attempt to increase the firepower of combat rifles—though none of these has been overly successful.

Magazine-fed repeating firearms made the old multibarreled firearms more or less obsolete; such weapons normally are seen only with expensive sporting drillings or with "survival" or hunting guns like the Savage 24. And the multibarreled experimental weapons seldom get out of the lab. But a few double guns—reincarnated in semiauto—are making a comeback in military and law-enforcement circles.

The most notable of these new guns is the M203 grenade launcher developed during the Vietnam War. Created around the AR-15/M16 rifle, it has generated spin-offs, including various types of shotguns (usually modified

Remington 1100s or 870s) mounted on the AR-15, and West German and Soviet 40mm grenade launcher/rifle combination weapons that borrow heavily from the M203.

But despite the fact that the semiauto action is generally as lightweight (or heavy, depending on your point of view) as many single-shot rifles, few auto loaders have ever been coupled together commercially for the civilian market, with the exception of the M203-style guns and AR-15/shotgun combinations. Many combinations that might be useful for the law-enforcement

An example of the almost unlimited variations of combination rifles that can be created around a Mini-14. This one uses steel brackets to hold a 10/22 (using a cut-down M1 Carbine stock) next to a Ranch Rifle with a Ram-Line folder. Eagle's 35-round magazine is in the Mini-14; a 50-round Ram-Line graces the 10/22.

and self-defense markets have never been developed.

But this doesn't mean it isn't practical for you to create such weapons yourself. Such a combination can give you the choice of two cartridges in the Mini-14—the powerful .223 cartridge and a shotgun, .22 LR, or 9mm Luger, for instance.

Such a semiauto combination gun can be ideal for combat where high rates of fire are called for or in hunting situations where various types of game might be encountered unexpectedly. (And of course it's great for getting strange looks at the rifle range!) It's very easy for the do-it-yourselfer to create such a useful combination around a number of guns, including the Mini-14 and Mini-30.

The secret to building such Frankenstein-like guns is in finding reliable methods of joining the two firearms. One way that works well with guns that have their gas systems above the barrel is based on a pair of brackets (like those manufactured by Choate Machine & Tool) normally used to secure extended shotgun magazines to their barrels. These can also be used to secure two barrels together so one gun hangs under the barrel of the other. This is a simple, inexpensive, and effective way to mount the many guns together.

It doesn't work well with the Mini-14, however, since its gas system is below the barrel. But there are other methods that are suited to the rifle. One way of mounting secondary firearms below the Mini-14's barrel or to the right side of the rifle is to use a different type of bracket. These are easy to construct from sheet metal using a hacksaw, file, and drill. By using four rectangular brackets, each having four screw holes (two for each gun being connected), it's possible to connect the stocks of a Mini-14 and Ruger 10/22 rifle or other firearm together securely. This method works with both plastic and wooden stocks and is easily removed if it's no longer needed. The system is very flexible, allowing you to mount guns side by side as well as above and below each other.

With plastic stocks, it's also possible to use a soldiering iron to "weld" the two stocks together as outlined in Chapter 1. Provided a number of strong seams are created, this will permanently unite the two stocks into one solid component. Of course, the catch to this is that you'll be committed to a combination gun—disconnecting the two stocks will be nearly impossible once they're consolidated.

Plastic welding should not be used with shotguns or the more heavily recoiling Mini-30 or larger-caliber rifles. The excessive recoil of some guns might cause a poorly done plastic weld to come loose or split. But the technique should work with .22 LR and .223 rifles if some time is taken to do a thorough job.

With side-by-side mounts, it's often possible to use the sights of each of the two firearms. But some combinations make using the sights of one or the other guns awkward if not impossible. There are several solutions to this problem.

One is to zero the second gun's barrel to the sights of the one most easily used. But this isn't easy, and getting the two barrels perfectly aligned entails tedious adjustments. Even when aligned, the different trajectories of the guns may cause them to be zeroed only at certain ranges.

Fortunately, there's a simple answer to aiming the second firearm. All that's needed is a scope and a see-through mount that can be placed above the sights. The see-through mount allows the iron sights to be used for one barrel, and the scope is then zeroed to the other gun.

A number of companies offer see-through mounts for the Mini-14 and Mini-30. The Armson OEG is available from L.L. Baston for $190 with such a mount; Eagle Industries has a quick-detach scope mount in black or stainless steel that accepts any 1-inch scope while allowing the use of the iron sights (cost is $50); and Ram-Line offers a tough polymer see-through mount that accepts any Weaver-style scope rings ($25).

It's also possible to mount a Mini-14 under some rifles if its stock is cut off just behind the receiver. In such a case, the 12-gauge shotgun magazine sling swivel base clamps ($5 each) from Choate may be useful. You can easily fabricate similar brackets from sheet metal by carefully measuring the distance that needs to be covered between the gun barrels. A ball peen hammer and scrap pipe can be used to bend the ends of the brackets so they will curve around the barrels of the guns to grip them tightly. A self-adjusting clamp can be created by joining the two sheet metal halves at their centers with one screw and nut. This makes it simple to tighten and thereby unite two barrels even if they have different diameters.

Since only one buttstock is needed for a double gun, you'll generally need to cut the stock off one or the other of the guns being created. This will make your double gun lighter and easy to carry.

Before permanently attaching guns or cutting off stocks, you'll need to give careful consideration to where ejection ports, charging levers, safeties, magazine releases, and triggers are located. The results of covering up any of these will be intolerable.

When experimenting with possible layouts of two firearms to be joined together, it's wise to use some duct tape to create a temporary combination gun. This will enable you to try the layout and determine whether you'll be creating a useful combination or an unwieldy monster you'll never really use. This can save a lot of time, effort, and money, and it should convince you of whether or not such a gun is suitable for you.

For those not wanting to cut up the wooden stock that comes with a firearm, the 10/22 rifle is ideal for adding to the Mini-14 since the little .22 rifle can be operated without its stocks.

To prepare the 10/22 for such operation, you need to

replace the two pins holding the trigger group to the receiver with bolts and nuts. And take care to be sure none of the cross pins are apt to come out (if they are loose, they can be secured with tape, or a sideplate held by the two replacement bolts holding the trigger group can be created to hold the pins in place). This "skeletal" 10/22 is lightweight and easy to mount to the Ruger. Furthermore, as we'll see in a subsequent chapter, the basic operation of the magazine release and safety can be modified on the 10/22 to make it nearly identical to the Mini-14 or Mini-30.

To cut one and a quarter pounds from the final weight of any combination gun using the 10/22, Ram-Line's steel-lined plastic Ultralight barrel ($39) can replace the steel barrel of the .22 rifle. The barrel is easily installed after loosening the two hex bolts holding the 10/22's barrel in place.

Because combination guns tend to be a bit heavy, you'll probably want to ease the burden of carrying your creation with a heavy sling worn in the assault position. As with the SAWs in the previous chapter, an M60 sling or one of Uncle Mike's modified for the assault carry with a shoelace or two seems to be ideal for this purpose.

The overall weight of the combination gun can be reduced further by removing unneeded hardware, and even further by using the standard 10-round magazine in the 10/22 and the 5-round magazine in the Mini-14 or Mini-30.

In combat or other situations where weight isn't a prime consideration, a Mini-14 combination rifle can create a lot of firepower through the use of large-capacity magazines.

Suppose, for example, you have a Mini-14 with a 10/22 connected to it. In such a case, you could use one of Ram-Line's $28 50-round magazines for the 10/22 (perhaps "jungle clipped" together since this works without much danger of getting dirt into them, thanks to the extreme quarter-circle curve they make). This would give you fifty shots before having to reload in the .22 LR half of your combination gun, with one hundred rounds available on this portion of the firearm if you've fastened two 50-round magazines together.

On the Mini-14 half of this gun, you could have a pair of 40-round magazines clipped together for 80 shots, or even carry a 90-round magazine to give 90 shots without reloading even once. With the jungle-clip arrangement of the 10/22 and a 90-Round Drum, the combination gun could fire 140 shots before a single magazine needs to be changed and holds 50 rounds in reserve!

If you're using the Mini-14 as the basis of an SAW, then even greater firepower is possible if you mount a second or third firearm to your unit. This is more practical with firearms being fired from fixed positions on a vehicle mount or tripod; the weight starts to become excessive as more guns are added to the combination weapon, making carrying it less and less practical.

In actual use, there are several ways a combination rifle can be fired. The actual method of firing will be determined in part by how the various firearms incorporated into the design are connected. Sometimes you'll have to move the shooting hand from one grip to another in order to reach the trigger of each half of the firearm. With other layouts, it may be possible to use one hand to fire one firearm and the other to shoot the second (this is more often practical with bipod or tripod mounts).

Whether a combination gun is realistically suited to self-defense is undoubtedly open to debate. But with modern combat tactics that demand high rates of firepower, the combination would seem to be a natural. And while the .22 LR isn't noted for its quick fight-stopping ability, it is capable of creating serious wounds within one hundred yards and could therefore be used to lay down suppressing fire. This would save the more powerful .223 half of the rifle so it could be used as needed with a full magazine ready for "serious work."

An additional advantage of using the .22 LR for some

types of combat, especially in urban areas, would be that stray shots would be less apt to penetrate walls and hurt innocent bystanders (of course, the .22 is still dangerous, and you would need to exercise judgment in densely populated areas).

Hunters or policemen with a combination gun might also load CCI's or Federal's CB Long cartridges into the .22 LR half of a combination gun. With nearly silent shots, the .22 CB Cap could be used to "neutralize" game or guard dogs, silently harass a barricaded opponent, or quietly extinguish floodlights in a brightly lit area.

The potential of silenced shots is great. The .22 CB Cap cartridges do have to be cycled through a semiauto action since they lack the power to operate the bolt, but this is a small price for the added flexibility they give a shooter. (For those using two 50-round Ram-Line magazines clipped together, one magazine might be filled with standard .22 LR cartridges and the other with .22 CB Caps. This would enable the shooter to slip the type of cartridges he needed into the rifle and cycle a cartridge into the chamber in just a few seconds.)

Single-shot, pump, or semiautomatic shotguns (provided they don't have a recoil spring in their stock) can all have their buttstocks shortened and be mounted with a Mini-14 or Mini-30. The main consideration is to avoid cutting the shotgun to less than its legal overall length of 26 inches. Among the first choices for combination gun use would be the Mossberg 500, Remington 870, and F.I.E.'s LAW-12, as well as F.I.E.'s single-shot Hamilton and Hunter. Given the similar safety set-up between the Mini-14 and the LAW-12, this would likely be a very good choice for many shooters.

Browning-type, recoil-operated shotguns whose barrels recoil slightly during the reloading cycle should *not* be used as combination guns wherein the barrel is secured to the other weapon, because this would keep them from functioning properly. Also, the stout recoil of the Browning action (used in most shotguns that are recoil-operated self-loaders) makes them less than ideal for most combination guns.

Whether semiauto, pump, or single-shot, a shotgun mounted on a combination gun can be turned into a mini-flamethrower with a Dragon's Breath shotgun cartridge (sold by Rhino Replacement Parts for $15.50 per pack of three rounds). Each of these cartridges creates a stream of burning metal powder that extends slightly beyond three hundred feet and lasts for three seconds. The flame is capable of blinding and causing minor burns to an enemy. It can also start fires and will definitely "light up" any area when fired. The first choice for such combination guns is F.I.E.'s cut-down SS version of its single-shot 12-gauge hunting shotguns.

Firearms aren't the only devices that can ride with a Mini-14 in a combination gun. One such thing is black-powder guns. Although these would be considered firearms by most of us, they aren't classified as such by BATF. Therefore, they don't fall under the legal limitations on barrel and overall length that govern standard firearms. Because of this, it's possible to create short-barreled shotguns (or even shot-filled pistols) with black-powder guns or to mount revolvers on the combination gun without running afoul of any laws in most areas (just be sure to check state and local regulations to be on the safe side).

One excellent candidate for a combination gun is Ruger's stainless steel Old Army revolver. Though modeled after the old Remington six-shooter, the Old Army has strengthened parts and coil springs, which make it far less apt to break than most other black-powder reproduction guns. The stainless steel also eases maintenance and cleaning of the revolver.

A wealth of other black-powder firearms are currently sold in the United States. Navy Arms and E.M.F. are two good sources of such guns. Take a trip to your local gunshop and you'll likely find a number of black-powder firearms that can easily be adapted to your combination gun.

Air guns can also be mounted on combination firearms. Daisy's CO_2 pellet guns like the Power Line 92 (which offers ten shots of .177 pellets without reloading), Power Line 44, and 1200 pistols all lend themselves to this. They would give you a quick and quiet way to deal with anything from unfriendly dogs to small pests. Like black-powder firearms, the overall length of air guns is generally unrestricted, so they can be mounted on a combination gun without legal problems in most areas of the United States.

You might also mount tear gas canisters or similar aerosol products, as well as paint guns (whose pellets could be filled with tear gas or other materials rather than paint) on a combination gun.

A little common sense must be exercised and thought given to just what the end result of mounting a nonfirearm on the combination gun will be. Will it really serve any purpose other than creating a strange-looking wall hanger? If not, perhaps you should rethink what you are doing.

Care must also be exercised not to cause those you are aiming at with tear gas, a pellet gun, or other nonlethal half of the combination gun to think the lethal portion of the firearm is about to be used on them. And as far as that goes, realize that having to aim the rifle in order to use the tear gas spray is an accident waiting to happen in many ways.

A good rule of thumb would be to point a combination gun at an antagonist or animal *only* if you're prepared to kill. If you can exploit the pellet gun or tear gas to frighten the man or animal off without actually using the firearm portion of your weapon, fine. But this way, if you do pull the wrong trigger, you won't have made a serious mistake.

CHAPTER 6

Of Families, Compatibles, and Modifications

Companies catering to the military market often try to create a family or weapons system based on one basic rifle design represented in carbine, rifle, SAW, LMG, or even GPMG forms (perhaps with a combination gun/grenade launcher version as well). Among the more notable of these are the Stoner 63 and Heckler & Koch's variations on the G3 rifle in 9mm, 7.62x39mm, .308, and .223, among other chamberings. (For a closer look at these weapons, see my book *Assault Pistols, Rifles, and Submachine Guns*, available from Paladin Press.)

What's the advantage of a family of rifles? A family of like-operating guns simplifies repair (when the firearms have common parts), makes learning/training with the gun quicker, and—during times of intense pressure when habits often take over—ensures that critical reflexes gained from operating one firearm don't become detrimental when applied to another weapon being carried. This latter point is of prime concern to many soldiers since flipping a nonexistent safety—or missing the one that's "in the wrong place"—can spell added danger or even death.

For much the same reason, many individuals also try to create a family of firearms for their own use. This allows habits formed with any of the firearms to carry over during a critical moment when reflexes and habits take over. It also allows the shooter to concentrate on hitting his target rather than fighting the firearm to get it to function properly.

Using the Mini-14 as the primary pattern for such a family, it's possible to amass a number of other guns that cover a variety of shooting tasks. For example, you could have a .22 conversion kit or 10/22 modified to operate like a Mini-14. A Mini-30 could then be added to fire 7.62x39mm as a short-range deer rifle (or a more powerful combat rifle). An M14, M1A, or Garand rifle could be purchased for the same overall layout of rifle to fire .308 or .30-06 cartridges. An F.I.E. LAW-12 would enable you to fire 12-gauge shotgun shells in a semiauto whose operating lever and safety operate just like those of the Mini-14.

You could add a Marlin Camp Carbine, Calico M-900, or Feather AT-9 carbine, which would enable you to shoot 9mm Luger or .45 ACP cartridges. And if you wanted to add an oversize pistol to your family of guns, then you could incorporate the Calico M-950. Such a collection of firearms would give a shooter a wide range of shooting capabilities and make it possible to choose a firearm to suit the task at hand.

About the only glaring hole in such a family of Mini-14-style firearms is in the area of handguns. While the Calico M-950 certainly fulfills the role from a ballistics standpoint, it's hardly a gun you'll carry in a belt holster. Neither is a pistol modification of the Mini-14 (even if you can get around the red tape to make one). A chopped AT-9 would come close to pistol proportions, though it would be nearly as heavy as the M-950 and, again, would involve a lot of red tape to fabricate since it is currently manufactured only as a carbine. And all three would be too big for holster carry, though they are comfortable on slings. So, if you're intent on creating a family of firearms and need the handiness of a pistol, you won't discover any handguns with ahead-of-the-trigger safeties like that of the Mini-14 in today's marketplace.

The need for a Mini-14-style safety is, however, somewhat of a "straw problem." In fact, the solution isn't too difficult to figure out: simply purchase a pistol that can be safely carried and fired without requiring you to release a safety.

This is just what a number of the new pistols do—and virtually all revolvers. The Ruger P-85, F.I.E. TZ-75 Series 88, Beretta/Taurus 92 series of guns, Colt Double Eagle, S&W autos, and Glock 17 can all be carried safely with the safety (if existent) in the fire position. This is perfectly safe since internal safeties keep the gun from firing if it's accidentally dropped while allowing a double-action first shot without doing anything other than pulling the trigger—provided a cartridge has been chambered beforehand. (For a closer examination of these guns, suggested modifications, and accessories, see my book *Automatics: Fast Firepower, Tactical Superiority*, available from Paladin Press.)

Revolvers are much the same, but they offer a wider choice of calibers and sizes. First choice among the revolvers are Ruger's new GP-100 series (in .38 Special/.357 Magnum), the "hide out" SP-101 (in .38 Special), and, for those wanting riflelike power in a handgun package, the .44 Magnum Super Redhawk. These revolvers cover a very wide gamut of cartridge powers; sources inside Ruger suggest that a .22 version of these guns may be forthcoming. (Readers interested in purchasing a revolver may find my book *Combat Revolvers: The Best (and Worst) Modern Wheelguns*, available from Paladin Press, to be of help when it comes to picking a wheelgun as well as the accessories for it.)

Aside from handguns, there are Mini-14-compatible rifles

and carbines in a wide range of calibers. Compatibility can be further enhanced by using similar stocks and sighting systems on all the family members. Ram-Line, for example, makes its plastic folder for the Ruger 10/22 and Marlin Camp Rifles (in 9mm and .45), the Mini-14 and Mini-30, as well as several of the Marlin rifles. Likewise, Muzzlelite bullpup stocks are available for the Mini-14, Mini-30, 10/22,

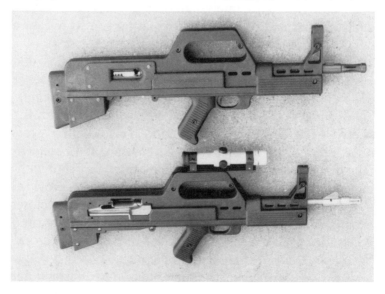

The Muzzlelite stocks lend themselves to creating a family of rifles. Shown here is a 10/22 with a Ram-Line Ultralite barrel and permanently-mounted flash hider (top) and a stainless Mini-14 with a Choate flash hider (bottom). Note the plastic scope mount that comes with all Muzzlelite stocks.

and Marlin Camp Rifles. The Falcon Folder is available for the Mini-30, Mini-14, Marlin Camp Rifles, and M1 Carbine. Choate makes folding and fixed stocks for the Mini-14, 10/22, and M1 Carbine. Any of these stocks would allow you to get very close to the same configuration on all your rifles and carbines for a standard feel and point of aim from one firearm to the next.

Now let's take a look at some of the firearms, as well as the accessories and modifications that can help them become similar to the Mini-14 in their operation.

AT-22

The AT-22 is an excellent .22 LR carbine that was designed by Jim Sullivan—one of the design team that worked on creating the AR-15 and later the Mini-14. Therefore, it isn't surprising that the AT-22 bears some of the attributes of both the AR-15 and the Mini-14. The AT-22 is currently marketed by Feather Enterprises.

The front sight of the AT-22, with a ring around its post, is similar to the Heckler & Koch rifles. If you've added one of the Eagle H&K-style sights to your Mini-14 or Mini-30, then you won't need to modify the AT-22. But if you have an M14-style sight with a post surrounded by dog ears (as offered by Choate in their combination front sight/flash hider), then you might want to cut off the top loop of the ring to leave dog ears on either side of the post. Coupled with the rear peep sight, this will make a sight picture very much like that of the AR-15.

If you have the standard Mini-14 front sight, you may wish to cut the ring off the AT-22 since this will give you the same single-post view that the Mini-14 has. The rear sight of the AT-22 is an excellent peep sight that gives a picture very similar to that of the Mini-14.

Several styles of pistol grips can be found on the AT-22. The original pistol grips were Ram-Line's Laser (A2-style) grips, modified slightly to fit the rifle. Newer guns have an AR-18/AR180-style grip unlike any found on the Mini-14 pistol-grip stocks made by other manufacturers. Therefore, you may wish to replace these with a Ram-Line or other grip in order to make the AT-22 more compatible with your Mini-14.

This conversion is relatively simple. The grip is removed

by taking out its screw. An AR-15A1- or A2-style grip can then be altered by cutting a small slot into its front to accommodate the trigger guard (use the old pistol grip as a guide). That done, the trigger guard fits into the slot, and the grip is easily remounted with its screw.

The magazine of the AT-22 holds twenty rounds, which is about right for a lightweight .22. Unlike that of the Mini-14, the release is located in front of the magazine rather than just ahead of the trigger guard. This is one difference that most shooters will probably have to live with, though it might be possible to fabricate an extension and silver-solder it onto the original. This would be a lot of work, however, and the results likely disappointing.

Fortunately, the two most important features of the AT-22, the charging lever and safety, are nearly identical to those of the Mini-14 in operation. The charging lever is on the right side of the receiver, and the safety is of the Garand/M14/Mini-14 style.

The barrel of the AT-22 is threaded to accept the AR-15 flash hider, so a wide range of styles is available (though a flash hider on a .22 LR gun is more cosmetic than useful). The telescoping stock of the AT-22 might also be removed and its mounting brackets and lock used to provide an anchor spot for a new solid stock if such were desired.

For a time, an AT-22 pistol version was manufactured by Feather Enterprises. Unlike chopped rifles, this was as easy to purchase as a standard .22 pistol because it was manufactured from the outset as a .22 pistol rather than as a rifle converted to a pistol (an important legal consideration).

There wasn't much of a market for the AT-22 pistol, however, and the wide variance of power among various loads of .22 LR ammunition contributed to some functioning problems with more anemic cartridges. But the pistol itself is excellent when used with quality ammunition. Therefore, those wanting a Mini-14-style .22 pistol might want to watch the used gun market and add one of these to their collection.

The AT-22 carbine has a 17-inch barrel that is easily removed by unscrewing the nut that's holding it. The gun weighs only 3.24 pounds unloaded. The AT-22 carbine, as well as its pistol spin-off, are excellent firearms that are well suited to use as the .22 LR member of a Mini-14 family of guns.

AT-9

Feather Enterprise's entry into the 9mm Luger market was marked by the introduction of the AT-9. The carbine has many of the design elements of the AT-22, including right-side charging lever, rear peep sight, H&K-style front sight, and a Mini-14-style safety at the forward end of the trigger guard.

The AT-9 weighs five pounds, which helps tame the recoil of the 9mm cartridge in its blowback system. About the only major difference between the AT-9 and the Mini-14 is in the magazine release (which is also different from the AT-22). The release is a button rather than a lever.

The AT-9 comes with a modified 25-round magazine similar to that of the Uzi. It's likely that a 32-round magazine may become available for the AT-9 in the future, and sources inside Feather Industries indicate that the company has been working on an extended-capacity drum magazine which may soon become available for the AT-9 (and other firearms).

A chopped version (short barrel/stockless) of the AT-9 would make a dandy assault pistol. If such a gun were manufactured by Feather Enterprises, it could be owned by nearly anyone—except those living in overly restrictive states like California or cities operating under a siege mentality. Unfortunately, Feather Enterprises doesn't have any plans to produce such a pistol, so only those willing to pay the special federal taxes and go through the legal red tape will be able to create one by chopping down a carbine's stock.

As with other carbines, the longer barrel of the AT-9 gives bullets more power than they would have if fired from a shorter pistol barrel. Even greater power can be realized by using high-power loads designed specifically for carbines. Among the best of these are Samson's 9mm Carbine loadings. These make the AT-9 considerably more potent than when it is used with standard ammunition.

Provided you can live with the slightly different magazine release, the AT-9 makes an excellent addition to the Mini-14 family and is a good firearm in its own right.

Calico M-900 and M-950

These rifles and assault pistols have a very "space-age" look, with lots of plastic and aluminum incorporated into their designs to keep them lightweight. Their styling makes them look very futuristic; not surprisingly they've already appeared in several sci-fi movies. But more important than that is the fact that they also work very well and have several design features that make them compatible with the Mini-14.

One major difference between the Calico guns and the Mini-14 is in the magazines. The Calico firearms feed from a "helical" magazine that has the cartridges stacked at the rear of the gun, over the receiver, in a spiral. Provided care is taken to wind the spring of the magazine properly, it functions quite well. And it has the added advantage of being able to store cartridges indefinitely with the spring relaxed. (A release button at the rear of the magazine makes it possible to remove the tension after it has been taken off the gun.)

There are three magazines available for the Calico 9mm guns. One holds one hundred rounds, the second holds twenty-nine, and the third holds fifty. These magazines will fit both the rifle and pistol versions of the gun.

Calico also markets an excellent reloading tool that

The Calico M-900 shown "decked out" in the accessories available for it. The company's scope mount has an Aimpoint 1000, a laser is mounted over the handguard, and the barrel sports the flash hider designed for it. The stock is in its forward position. (Photo courtesy of Calico.)

The Calico M-900 loader makes it possible to load the company's 50-round magazine in just seconds from the time it takes to open the box of ammunition until the magazine is full. Note the winding lever on the magazine, which is in its unfolded position. (Photo courtesy of Calico.)

allows a box of cartridges to be deposited into the magazines about as quickly as they can be fired. This is a good investment for those who will do a lot of practicing.

The carbine version of this firearm is the M-900, and a "jazzed up" version with forward pistol grip and muzzle brake is being sold as the M-951. The pistol version is designated the M-950 (originally dubbed the M-900P). Sources at Calico say that a .223 carbine version of the firearm is also in the works, though it isn't slated to be released commer-

The Calico M-950 pistol with its 50-round magazine in place. The Staggered helical magazine above the M-950 fits either the carbine or pistol and carries one hundred rounds of ammunition. (Photo courtesy of Calico.)

cially until the mid-1990s. The tentative model designation for the .223 rifle will be the M-23; only a 100-round magazine is slated to be produced for it.

For military and police users, selective-fire models of the 9mm guns are available. The M-950A is the machine pistol version; it has a short barrel, is stockless, and has a forward pistol grip to aid in control when shooting. The M-950A has a short barrel and stock. (Since the forward pistol grip is easily removed from the foregrip, it seems likely that versions of these various models with and without the grip will be seen often.)

The safeties on all of the 9mm guns are similar to those of the Mini-14; they lie at the front of the trigger guard where they can be flicked on or off with the trigger finger. The charging lever is located on the left rather than the right of the gun, but this is easy to adapt to since it is operated in the same manner as that of the Mini-14.

The tough glass-filled polymer and aluminum used in the Calico guns makes them amazingly light. The M-900 carbine only weighs 7.2 pounds with its 16-inch barrel and folding stock *and* a loaded 100-round magazine; it weighs only 2.25 pounds empty (about the same as a Colt 1911 auto pistol).

An H&K-style locking system is another reason for the gun's light weight. Not only does this keep the bolt light, it also tames the recoil. In addition to the fact that the pistol grip is nearly in line with the barrel, recoil is very mild. An added plus of the locking system is that the empty brass (ejected out of the bottom of the receiver) comes out very gently. This makes it nearly impossible to have a finger or hand hurt if they inadvertently get in the way of the ejection port (something that can be said of few other firearms).

A few shooters may find the telescoping stock of the M-900 carbine a tad uncomfortable. It would be rather easy, however, to replace it with a fixed wooden stock—a job some do-it-yourselfers may wish to tackle.

The notched-style rear sight is attached to the top of the magazine. This, too, is readily changed by creating a peep sight from scrap metal. The new peep sight can be mounted on the existing sight with epoxy cement. It's simple to make sight adjustments on the Calico guns with two finger-controlled wheels located near the front

Three Franchi shotguns imported by F.I.E. *Left*: The SAS-12. Operating with a slide, it isn't as ideal as the other two guns for a Mini-14 family of firearms. *Center*: The LAW-12. *Right*: The SPAS-12. (Photo courtesy of F.I.E.)

sight post at the front of the magazine.

Calico offers a number of accessories for its 9mm guns, including short and long muzzle compensators, a laser-mount rail (that rides over the handguard), a forward pistol grip, brass catchers, and an excellent scope mount.

The Calico guns are very well made and well designed. For those looking for a 9mm gun compatible with the Mini-14, the M-900 and M-950 merit consideration.

F.I.E. LAW-12 and SPAS-12

The Franchi LAW-12 and SPAS-12 are imported to the United States by F.I.E. Both guns share a number of accessories, including a standard sporting stock, a fixed pistol-grip wooden stock, a folding stock (which has an optional carrying handle when folded), and a pistol-grip stock with detachable buttstock. Choate Machine & Tool also offers a skeletonized plastic stock that can be mounted on either shotgun. Screw-in chokes, a shot-spreader attachment, and a scope mount are also available from F.I.E.

Both shotguns are capable of taking a lot of abuse and can fire a wide range of loads (though, for best operation, the loads recommended by the manufacturer should be used). The SPAS-12 was created in the early 1980s with an eye toward military and police sales. It is rather heavy (9.6 pounds empty) due to the fact that it has a foregrip that can be used to manually cycle loads through the magazine, effectively converting the gun from semiauto to a pump-action shotgun. The LAW-12 operates only in a semiauto mode and is relatively lightweight (7.5 pounds). It's considerably simpler to operate since the conversion button to switch to manual operation is missing, as is the pump assembly.

Both guns have two manual safeties located at the front of the trigger guard. One, the quick-employment safety, works in a manner similar to that of the Mini-14; coupled with the right-side charging lever, this safety makes the

LAW-12 an ideal addition to a family of Mini-14-style firearms. (The SPAS-12, because of its complexity and heavier weight, won't be for everyone, though it may appeal to some shooters looking for a gun capable of handling a wide range of shotgun shells.)

The second safety on these shotguns is more awkward to operate and is generally better left off if you need to shoot in a hurry (say in hunting or self-defense). On older models, this second safety is a lever that must be rotated 180 degrees to get from safe to fire position. Newer guns have a cross-bolt safety.

The barrels of the LAW-12 and SPAS-12 are 21.5 inches long. The magazine under the barrel of each shotgun holds eight shells. Interestingly, it's possible to actually carry ten shells in the gun, ready to go. This is due to an excellent design that allows the shotgun to chamber a shell even if it gets caught behind the shell lifter. In addition to making it impossible to jam a gun if a shell fails to get locked into the magazine (something that can happen during combat or other tense situations), this design also allows a shell to be placed in the chamber, eight more in the magazine, and a tenth just above the lifter. This gives the shotgunner a fantastic amount of firepower before he needs to reload. (For hunting, a rod can be placed in the magazine to limit the shotgun's capacity to any legal limitations on magazine size.)

The SPAS-12 has a notched rear sight and large blade at the front, which work fairly well. The LAW-12 has a single sight post, but many shooters may find the stock makes using the sight rather awkward. Do-it-yourselfers might choose to work on raising the sight or reworking the stock. Those looking for a quick fix should purchase the scope mount available for the shotgun and place an electric dot scope on it.

Most people will find the carrier latch button on these shotguns aggravating because it must be depressed to load the magazine. This can make the already slow task of reloading even slower. Fortunately, a gunsmith can cure this problem easily.

The stocks on the SPAS-12 and LAW-12 also lack a rubber recoil pad. While the gas action of the shotguns eats up some of the recoil, the guns can still be punishing to shoot with full shotgun loads. Therefore, shooters may wish to add a recoil pad to the stock, using the methods outlined in Chapter 2. This will make either gun much more pleasant to shoot. (Needless to say, the metal folding stock is unpleasant to shoot and is generally better avoided unless it's essential for storage purposes.)

The LAW-12 (but not the SPAS-12) was banned from being imported into the United States in the late 1980s as part of an ill-conceived way of keeping guns out of the hands of drug dealers (even though it's doubtful that many, if any, of these guns have been used by such people). Nevertheless, a number of them can still be found in the United States and, hopefully, they will be imported again in the near future.

Garand

The M1 Garand rifle was perfected by John Garand at the Springfield Armory after sixteen years of development. In 1936, the U.S. Army adopted the rifle, which became the M1. It served American soldiers well through World War II and the Korean War.

Large numbers of Garands were manufactured by American allies overseas. During the mid-1980s, laws restricting the importation of military surplus firearms were relaxed, allowing many of these now-obsolete military guns into the United States. They carry a low price tag and are generally in good to passable shape. As such, they make good semiauto hunting rifles, though they are a bit heavy (9.5 pounds empty) and long (43.5 inches) by modern standards.

The Garand uses an 8-round clip (not a magazine) that's thrown from the rifle with its last shot—a unique attribute that many dislike, though it does speed up reloading. Fortunately, clips are relatively cheap so occasionally losing one in the grass isn't too great a tragedy.

The Garand uses the old .30-06 cartridge, making it powerful enough for any game animal encountered in North America. The safety is nearly identical to that of the Mini-14 (though generally a bit harder to operate), and the charging handle is in the same position. The rear sight is the standard military peep sight, making it ideal for Mini-14 users needing the power of this cartridge.

Occasionally, chamber inserts are used to convert the Garand to .308. Don't try this yourself or purchase such a rifle, since inserts have a way of coming out with empty brass. Chambering and firing a cartridge in the then-too-large chamber could wreck the gun—and you. Stick with the .30-06 version.

M1A/M14

Shortly after World War II, Lloyd Corbett, working at the U.S. Springfield Armory, altered the M1 Garand slightly into what became known as the T44 configuration. After a series of tests and improvements, the U.S. Army adopted the T44 as its M14 rifle in 1957.

The modifications to the Garand consisted of adding a 20-round detachable box magazine (rather than the 8-round clip), moving the gas port back eight inches to help improve accuracy, and lessening the abrupt recoil of the rifle, along with other minor design improvements. While this resulted in a good rifle, it turned out that many design features weren't really what the army was looking for.

One of the problems with the new M14 was that is wasn't easily controlled in the automatic mode, thanks to the recoil of the powerful .308 Winchester/7.62mm NATO cartridge

for which it was chambered. As far as the army was concerned, this made it less than ideal and various new muzzle brakes and rifle stocks did little to cure this problem. Consequently, the rifle was soon retired and replaced by the M16 in .223. Only the scoped, rebarreled version of the M14 remained in service as the M21 sniper rifle, though many M14s were stockpiled for some time and made their way to National Guard units as well as to American allies overseas.

Like the Garand, the M14 rifle and its spin-offs are ideal for those accustomed to the Mini-14 since the safety, charging lever, and sights are virtually identical to those of the Mini-14. Additionally, the magazine release of the M14 is indistinguishable from that of the Mini-14, which was modeled after the older rifle.

Probably the most notable of the civilian models of the M14

Springfield Armory's M1A, decked out with an ART IV target scope and cammo Kevlar stock. As can be seen from this photo, the basic layout of this .308 rifle is nearly identical to that of the Mini-14, making this a good addition to a "family" of rifles. (Photo courtesy of Springfield Armory.)

137

currently available are those made by the Springfield Armory. The company makes its own parts and receivers and actually produces a rifle better than the one that was fielded for the U.S. Army.

Several models of this rifle are offered by Springfield Armory. Among them are the standard semiauto M1A, the M1A-A1 (a short-barreled version available with or without a folding stock), and the M14 (or M1A) decked out with the M14A1 (also known as the E2) stock.

Two versions of the M1A available from Springfield Armory. The top gun is mounted on an E2 stock; note forward grip and hinged buttplate, both designed to aid in controlling the rifle. The bottom M1A-A1 has a shortened barrel and the BM-59-style stock.

Those having a Mini-14 with a pistol grip will undoubtedly find the M14A1-style stock more to their liking. So will shooters with smaller hands, because the E2 stock is more comfortable than that of the standard M14, which has a larger grip. The folding stocks originally designed for the BM-59/62 (the modified Garand developed by the Italians, which is nearly identical to the M14) are also available for the M1A rifles. These are good, if heavy, stocks, though some shooters will dislike the trigger position, which is rather high with these stocks in place.

The Springfield Armory rifles are manufactured with a 1-in-10 twist for lighter .308 bullets and with a 1-in-12 twist for heavier bullets. Care should be taken to fire only the weight of bullet specified for the rifle, as heavier loads can sometimes damage the gas system.

In addition to the standard 20-round magazine, Springfield Armory offers 5- and 10-round magazines for hunting. Magazines can be filled using the standard procedure of sticking in a round at a time from a stripper clip and guide, or with a stripper clip and guide machined into the top of the rifle's receiver.

Like the M1 Garand, the rear sight of the M14 can be adjusted with the fingers to compensate for both windage and elevation. This is good, provided care is taken not to lose track of where zero is (a dab of paint may help). Also like the Garand, many of these guns have a safety that's difficult to operate; a visit to the gunsmith will help with this problem.

A wide variety of accessories, from bayonets to winter triggers and winter safeties, are available for the M14. Magazines are also inexpensive, thanks to a large surplus market.

The M1A weighs 8.5 pounds (this varies with the stock), and the overall length is 44 inches.

M1 Carbine

The M1 Carbine was produced during World War II as a sort of replacement for the .45 automatic pistol, which was difficult to manufacture quickly. In fact, the M1 Carbine went well beyond its original role as a pistol replacement; more than six million were manufactured and went to all kinds of troops in Europe and the Pacific. The lightweight gun quickly became popular with American soldiers, despite the fact that its cartridge—coupled with the FMJ bullet required by the conventions of war—was rather ineffective.

The prototype fabricated by inventor "Carbine" Williams (working from a prison cell after being jailed for moonshining) was adopted in September 1941. Soon the M1 Carbine was being made by everyone from General Motors to Winchester to IBM in an effort to meet the demand for more weapons to be placed in the hands of American and Allied troops.

Following the Korean War, the M1 Carbine was gradually phased out of U.S. military arsenals, though it was still sometimes seen in the hands of troops in Vietnam and was popular with Third World countries receiving U.S. military aid. Consequently, huge numbers of these guns can still be found in warehouses around the world.

During the mid-1980s, legislation allowing military-surplus firearms to be imported into the United States brought in huge numbers of M1 Carbines. This, coupled with earlier commercial production and U.S. military sales, has placed a large number of these firearms on the military surplus and used gun markets in the United States. Consequently, these weapons carry price tags far below the quality of their workmanship and design.

The M1 Carbine has a peep sight and right-side charging handle coupled with the "feel" of the Mini-14. Its ahead-of-the-trigger safety is only somewhat similar to that of the Mini-14, but a skilled do-it-yourselfer can alter and enlarge the safety so it operates nearly like that of the Mini-14.

The magazine release is another story. It bears more resemblance to the AR-15 release than that of the Mini-14. It's possible to silver-solder a small bar to the release so it extends downward behind the magazine. In this configuration, it can then be released with the thumb, though the motion will be more side-to-side than forward as on the Mini-14.

The front sight of most M1 Carbines is a post with dog ears. This makes it compatible with many Mini-14s with aftermarket sights/flash hiders; the dog ears can also be removed for a single-post picture or a ring can be fabricated and silver-soldered to them for the "H&K look."

Choate Machine & Tool offers a fixed pistol-grip stock as well as a folder for the M1 Carbine. Both are nearly identical to the tough Zytel stocks Choate offers for the Mini-14 and 10/22, making them ideal for those creating a compatible version of the M1 Carbine. The folding stock costs $68, and the fixed stock is $45; those wanting a Nitex-finish folder to match stainless-steel versions of the M1 Carbine can get one for $80.

While the M1 Carbine is certainly light (5.5 pounds) and handy (35.7 inches), its biggest shortcoming is its cartridge. Falling between most pistol cartridges and the .223 Remington in power, it is, in many ways, a solution looking for a problem. After all, whether you're interested in hunting medium-sized game or self-defense work, both are better handled by the .223. At the other end of the scale, small game is taken more cheaply with the .22 LR or 9mm Luger cartridge. Thus, most shooters will be better off buying a .22 LR or saving their money and using the Mini-14 or .22 LR rifle for tasks the M1 Carbine might tackle marginally.

A few M1 Carbines are chambered for the 9mm Luger as well as the 5.7mm Johnson (also known as the .22 Spitfire). These versions were introduced in the 1960s and 1970s and are very similar to the standard M1 Carbines. The 5.7mm Johnson is especially attractive as a combat cartridge since it has the overall length of the standard .30 carbine cartridge while being necked down to hold a 40-grain .22-caliber cartridge. This gives it a muzzle velocity of around 2,800 fps, making it effective for close combat. An additional plus is that the standard 15- and 30-round magazines, bolt, and so forth of the .30-caliber M1 Carbine work in the 5.7mm version—only the barrel needs to be changed. Unfortunately, since it isn't offered commercially by any of the ammunition manufacturers due to the scant numbers of M1 Carbines chambered for it, this superior cartridge has to be custom-made and loaded by the shooter.

There is also a pistol version of the M1 Carbine. Marketed as the Enforcer by Iver Johnson, it has the receiver assembly of the standard rifle in a cut-down pistol-grip assembly lacking any buttstock. The barrel is 10.5 inches long (in contrast to the carbine's 16 inches), making it short and handy. Weighing in at 4 pounds with an overall length of 18.5 inches, this is a rather awkward "pistol" at best. The .30 Carbine cartridge loaded with a hollow-point bullet (a loading that is, unfortunately, difficult to find commercially) is more potent than the .357 Magnum cartridge, making the Enforcer a formidable, if somewhat awkward, weapon.

If you need that much power in a short package, you might be better off with a Mini-14 in a Muzzlelite bullpup stock. This would create a weapon that could be shouldered and aimed comfortably and would only be a few inches longer. Additionally, you could fire the more potent .223 cartridge, which has a better track record of effectiveness in combat.

So, when it's all said and done, the M1 Carbine can be used to fill in a gap in power between the .223 and 9mm cartridges. The problem is the gap isn't really in need of being filled for most shooters.

Marlin Camp Carbines

In 1985, Marlin added the Model 9 Camp Carbine to its lineup of sporting carbines and rifles. The rifle fires the 9mm Luger pistol cartridge and has traditional lines except for a magazine well that extends below its stock. This extended well was necessary to accommodate the pistol magazines the company elected to use.

While this gave the carbine a rather odd look, it made sense

from a design standpoint because it reduced the manufacturing needs of creating a magazine for the gun and also created a firearm that would use the same magazines many shooters might already own (those for the Smith & Wesson 59, 459, 559, and 669 series of automatics).

In 1986, Marlin introduced a sister firearm, the Model 45, to its lineup. This is nearly identical to the Model 9 except that it's chambered for the .45 auto pistol cartridge and employs magazines designed for the 1911 series of pistols.

The charging lever and safety of these two Marlin rifles are nearly identical to those of the Mini-14 in operation, making the rifles ideal additions to a family of firearms. Each sports a 16.5-inch barrel, and their receivers are tapped for easy addition of scope mounts to either carbine. The wooden stocks come with a rubber buttpad.

The carbines unfortunately

The Marlin Camp Carbine (shown here is the Model 45) makes an ideal companion to the Mini-14. The receiver is drilled for easy scope mounting. Like the Mini-14, the Camp Carbine's safety is ahead of the trigger and its charging handle is to the right of the receiver.

have sights that are different from the Mini-14. The front sight has a hooded post (giving a picture somewhat like the H&K front sight), while the rear sight is an open notch. But it's easy to convert these. The hood of the front sight is easily removed, and a peep sight can be improvised out of scrap metal and silver-soldered onto the rear sight without much work. Or you can simply mount a scope onto the rifle, if you have one on the Mini-14, to make the firearms compatible.

The magazine release is also a bit of a problem in terms of being different from the Mini-14's. The release is a button similar to that of most auto pistols, and it is located on the left side of the gun at the front of the magazine well. Many shooters may simply learn to live with this. Others may want to try extending the release with a piece of scrap metal soldered onto it (which won't be too satisfactory aesthetically or in operation).

Ram-Line offers a plastic folder for the Camp Carbines for $60; the company's $25, 18-round (MAW9117) magazine will also work well in the 9mm carbine. Eagle offers their Alpha-Mag that will fit in the Model 45 Camp gun; this magazine holds nine rounds and costs $32.

Like the AT-9, the Marlin Camp Carbines give bullets fired from them added velocity because of their longer barrels. Even greater velocity can be realized by using ammunition that's designed for carbines, such as Samson's 9mm and .45 ACP Carbine loads. Uzi and other brands of "+P" ammunition can also be used in the Camp Carbines. In effect, these cartridges will give "magnum" performance with standard chamberings.

At the time of this writing, there are rumors that Marlin is going to drop these rifles from its lineup. Even if this happens, many readers should be able to find these guns for some time and will do well to consider adding them to their collection of Mini-14-style firearms.

Sturm, Ruger 10/22

The Ruger 10/22 is very possibly one of the most dependable .22 rifles ever made. In addition to the 10-round magazine the rifle comes with, there are aftermarket extended magazines. Ram-Line currently offers a 50-round magazine for $25.

Another of Ram-Line's products, the Kwik Release, is ideal for making the 10/22 more like the Mini-14. For just $4, the Kwik Release replaces the magazine release to create a thumb-activated lever like that of the Mini-14 magazine release.

The 10/22's charging lever and stock are nearly identical to those of the Mini-14. The safety ahead of the 10/22's trigger is of a cross-bolt type, but this is capable of being altered to a Mini-14-style safety by cutting small grooves into its cylinder and silver soldering a metal safety plate onto the button. That done, the safety can be flicked off with the same motion used on the Mini-14. (It will be necessary to remove a small amount of wood from the stock to allow for easy field-stripping.)

For those who have a Mini-14 with a dog-eared front sight, L.L. Baston offers a slip-on hider with dog ears for $16. It's mounted on the rifle by simply drifting out the standard front sight and then slipping on the replacement.

As part of its Zepher 2200 assembly kit, Eagle Manufacturing offers an H&K-style ringed front sight/flash hider that's nearly identical in layout to the company's Mini-14 front sight. The kit also comes with an adjustable peep sight that mounts on the receiver of the 10/22. The kit costs $34.

Eagle also offers a QD (quick-detach) Scope-Mount kit that comes with Zepher 2200-style front and rear sights. The quick-detach scope mount accommodates a 1-inch scope (this is warranted, with the accuracy of most 10/22 rifles). Cost for the kit, including scope mount and sights, is $60.

Side by side comparison of Eagle's Zepher front sight/flash hider for the 10/22 (top) and the one it offers for the Mini-14 (bottom). The two sights are nearly identical, which would give the shooter the same picture when switching from one gun to the other.

Zepher 2200 Sighting System for the 10/22 can be modified to closely resemble the Mini-14's sights. The rear sight is an adjustable peep sight while the front is an H&K-style ringed post. (Photo courtesy of Eagle Manufacturing.)

Unfortunately, the 10/22 doesn't come from Sturm, Ruger & Company with peep sights. However, a do-it-yourselfer can fabricate a small peep sight from scrap metal and then replace the rear sight blade held in place by two tiny screws. Once done, this creates the sight picture of the Mini-14 for a very small investment of time.

Some shooters may also wish to add a plastic stock like that used on their Mini-14. Choate Machine & Tool offers a fixed and a folding stock ($50 and $72); Ram-Line sells its folder for $53; the Falcon Folder (from Adventurer's Outpost) costs $135 (blued) or $150 (stainless); and Muzzlelite offers its bullpup stock that's nearly identical to its Mini-14 stock for $97.

It should be noted that if the Ultralite barrel is used with the 10/22, it will cut a pound off the weight of what is normally a five-pound rifle. But extreme care must be exercised when mounting a 16-inch barrel on the 10/22 if it is used in

This 10/22 is encased in a Muzzlelite bullpup stock. A Ram-Line 50-round magazine, Ultralite barrel, and slip-on flash hider complete the system, which operates nearly identically to a Mini-14 mounted on a similar stock.

the bullpup configuration; it will be below the legal limit unless a flash hider or some other method is used to extend the overall length of the gun. Ram-Line offers a slip-on flash hider ($16) that will bring most bullpups to the required 26-inch overall length when mounted on the barrel.

To mount this flash hider to the plastic barrel permanently, drill a small detent in the barrel where the set screw will rest, then tighten the screw after adding a drop of Loctite to its threads. Once set, fill in the hole with epoxy glue or use a drill to cut off the hex nut opening in the top of the screw and seal the hole with epoxy. This will make the flash hider impossible to remove without cutting or grinding it off, thereby satisfying the legal criterion of not being easily converted to a shorter-than-legal length.

Ram-Line's Take Down Barrel Kit ($28) makes it possible to remove the barrel of the 10/22 by simply loosening a knob and pulling it out the front of the receiver. This greatly simplifies cleaning.

The Take Down Barrel Kit only fits in the Ram-Line stocks. However, by cutting out wood or plastic on the inside of the standard Ruger or other aftermarket stocks with wood chisels and a mallet, it's possible to make enough room to accommodate the kit.

With a wealth of accessories and a dependable design, the Ruger 10/22 makes an excellent .22 LR addition to the Mini-14 family of guns. (For a more detailed look at the history, variations, and accessories available for the 10/22, see my book *The Sturm, Ruger 10/22 Rifle and .44 Magnum Carbine*, available from Paladin Press.)

CHAPTER 7

Targeting Systems

ron sights were pretty well perfected by the late 1800s. Most of today's sights are little better in terms of design or performance, though materials and methods of fabricating them have certainly improved.

This is not true of optical sights, which have improved steadily throughout the twentieth century. Therefore, it's not surprising that telescopic sights are found on modern sporting rifles more and more often, and that the current trend in military weapons seems to be toward optical sights as well.

Iron sights have a definite advantage when it comes to toughness and price. And quality iron sights can be nearly as accurate as expensive scopes (though it's harder to be sure just what is being fired upon at extreme ranges without a scope).

Unlike many sporters, the Mini-14 has a rear peep sight. This type of sight is considerably more accurate than the V- or U-notch styles. And unlike the notch sights, the peep sight is forgiving to older eyes and considerably faster to bring into action. About the only advantage of the V- and

U-notch sights is that they're cheap to manufacture (which is why most sporters have them).

The peep sight is fast because it doesn't have to be in focus for the shooter to get it lined up with his front sight. Instead, the peep sight takes advantage of the eye's natural tendency to center the front sight in the brightest point—the center—of the peep sight. This "human-engineering feature" makes it possible for most shooters to get the front and rear sights lined up by reflex. The long sight radius of the Mini-14, with the rear sight at the back of the receiver and the front sight at the end of the barrel, is an added plus that lends accuracy to the rifle's iron sights.

The sights on the Ranch Rifle models of the Mini-14 and Mini-30 are hard to adjust accurately except with the "by-guess-and-by-golly" method of firing at a target, loosening

The Ranch Rifle version of the Mini-14 is ideal for scope mounting thanks to its integral scope mounts. The iron sights can be retained for emergency use should the scope become damaged. (Photo courtesy of Sturm, Ruger & Company.)

Close-up view of the Ranch Rifle's rear sight, showing its adjustment screws. Shown here is the Mini-30 sight, which is nearly identical to that of the Mini-14 Ranch Rifle. (Photo courtesy of Sturm, Ruger & Company.)

sight screws, and adjusting the sight. (This isn't much of a problem, however, since the iron sights simply act as emergency backup systems for the scope mounted on the receiver.)

For those who won't be mounting a scope on the Ranch Rifle, there's a simple fix that gives the shooter an excellent hooded peep sight with positive windage and elevation adjustments. The solution comes in the form of Williams' WGRS receiver sight that fits into the dovetail notch cut for the Ranch Rifle's rear sight. Installation is easy: simply drift out the old rear sight and drift in the WGRS. This sight is available from Brownells (product #962-100-143 WGRS-Mini 14/30) for $25; it fits either the Mini-14 Ranch Rifle or the Mini-30.

With other models of the Mini-14, the rear sight can be adjusted more precisely. With each click of the sight wheels, these peep sights change the point of impact by 1.5 inches at one hundred yards. Turning the side wheel counterclockwise moves the point of impact to the right; twisting the top adjustment wheel counterclockwise raises the point of impact.

A small punch or similar tool is ideal for releasing the

detent that holds the sight wheels in place. For really quick sight adjustments, a Mini-14 Sight Tool is available for $9 from L.L. Baston. It consists of a knurled knob with small projections that fit over the detent points of the sight wheel. Once pushed onto the sight wheel, it's simple to turn it the number of clicks you need to zero the rifle to the target.

The sight of the standard Mini-14 offers fine enough adjustment to zero the rifle, given the 3- to 4-inch groups it normally fires. However, for those with "accurized" versions of the gun, a finer adjustment may be desirable. Fortunately, there's a quick way to change to a finer adjustment providing .75-inch changes in point of impact at one hundred yards.

To create this adjustment, simply use a small round file to cut extra notches between each of those that already exist on the wheels. All you need is time and patience; provided the cuts are shaped so they're nearly identical to the originals on either side of them, the results will be satisfactory.

The size of peep aperture that comes with the Mini-14 is a very good compromise for both bright- and low-light viewing. However, these can be a bit hard to see through at times. When light is falling onto the rear surface of the sight, it creates a glare that causes the iris of the eye to close somewhat, thereby obscuring the sight picture.

The solution to this problem is the hooded-aperture sight. It will keep light from glaring off the sight, providing a bright sight picture that is surrounded by a high-contrast dark ring. Eagle Manufacturing offers a hooded replacement sight for the standard Mini-14 for just $3.

For those using the Ranch Rifle models of the Mini-14 and Mini-30, the WGRS sight mentioned above is the easiest way to add a hooded aperture. With a little effort, you can also fabricate a hooded-aperture sight from scrap metal and then solder it to the sight blade. Before soldering the hood to it, remove the sight blade by loosening the screws that hold it. Carefully file excess solder off the hood and blade and then darken the remaining solder with touch-up blue to match the sight.

Iron sights are very durable and light; they're quick to use, and are nearly oblivious to moisture, dirt, or temperature extremes. Whether you're using the Mini-14 for hunting, self-defense, or even target shooting, you'll probably find that with the correct sight aperture and a little practice estimating ranges, your rifle is as accurate as you can shoot. Shooters should think long and hard before adding the weight and complexity of a scope to their Mini-14.

Some people will benefit from a scope. For twilight shooting, the light-gathering qualities of some scopes are useful. And some people feel more confident if they can see their targets better through magnification.

For those who want or need a scope, there's a wealth of quality optical equipment to choose from. In picking one, you need to think about exactly what you'll be using your Mini-14 for and what jobs you want the scope to handle.

Among the variables to consider before purchasing a scope are its field of view (a wide field is good for hunting or self-defense but isn't necessary for target shooting), ruggedness (important for hunting or self-defense), weight (bearing in mind that lighter scopes will have decreased field of view and light-gathering qualities), and the light-gathering qualities (the more light a scope gathers, the darker the environment in which the rifle can be used accurately).

If you wish to mount a scope on the Mini-14, the Ranch-Rifle style is first choice since it does away with the need to purchase and mount the scope block. This model also helps prevent problems down the road since the Ranch Rifle's design is rugged and simple and the scope won't come loose because it's molded into the top of the receiver.

About the only time the Ranch Rifle scope mounts create problems is when a scope needs to be farther forward or backward than the ring positions allow for proper eye relief.

Close-up view of the Ranch Rifle scope mounting system. The rings screw onto studs molded to the top of the receiver, assuring alignment and a steady base for the scope. (Photo courtesy of Sturm, Ruger & Company.)

B-Square offers a mount that fits the standard Mini-14 rifle. The small knob makes it possible to remove the scope quickly if necessary. Shown here is an old Mark-V electric dot scope. (Photo courtesy of B-Square.)

(This is especially apt to happen with stocks that have longer lengths of pull or when compact scopes are used.) Fortunately, B-Square has created a mount that solves this problem. The mount (stock #16024), which sells for $50, clamps right onto the Ranch Rifle's dovetails and then allows a variety of scopes to be secured onto the base with Weaver-type mounts.

Eagle's QD scope mount comes complete with rings. The small lever allows the mount to be tightened or released easily. (Photo courtesy of Eagle Manufacturing.)

To mount a scope on the standard Mini-14 you'll need a mounting system, and there are a bunch to choose from. Among the best are the Eagle Manufacturing and Ram-Line quick-detach scope mounts. Aimpoint makes stainless and blued mounts for $53 each, and B-Square offers the Dovetail/NATO Stanag mount that accepts standard Weaver-style scope rings, as well as the variety of scopes and night-vision equipment with European-standard NATO Stanag mounts. Prices for the B-Square mounts are

$70 for blued finish and $80 for stainless steel.

As far as the scopes that will be placed on the mounts go, there's a huge number suitable for use on a Mini-14. Redfield, Leupold, Beeman, Tasco, Simmons, Bushnell, Shepherd, and so on, all offer tough scopes and back them with excellent service and warranties. Avoid purchasing little-known bargain scopes. These aren't usually very good buys; it's safer to stick with name brands when it comes to purchasing a scope.

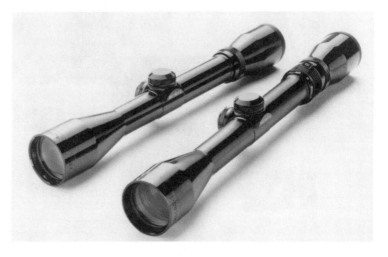

When purchasing scopes for the Mini-14, it is best to stick with name brands in order to ensure quality. Shown here are two excellent scopes from Weaver. (Photo courtesy of Weaver.)

Variable-power scopes offer more flexibility, but they are often plagued with frailties not found in optics that have fixed powers. In theory, variable scopes don't change the point of impact as the magnification is changed; in practice this isn't always so. Occasionally you'll find a scope whose point of aim will wander as the power setting is changed. Fortunately, major manufacturers will repair or replace scopes (usually free of charge) whose zero wanders as the magnification setting is changed. So when you purchase a variable scope, test it out right away and then return or exchange it if it doesn't hold its zero.

Variable scopes do have some pluses that make many shooters willing to put up with their frailties. At lower settings, you have a wide field of view so targets are more quickly engaged; higher settings can be used to inspect a target and give a shade more accuracy.

For all-round shooting, the 4X and 6X scopes seem to be the best compromises. Over the years, everyone from snipers to hunters has come to the conclusion that this range of power is most ideally suited to quick shooting where magnification is needed.

Beyond 6X, the field of view shrinks to the point that it's hard to find moving targets, and the wobble introduced by the human nervous system as well as the wind and environment make the target appear shaky. Therefore, unless you're trying to plug small varmints or stationary targets from great distances, you probably won't need some of the more powerful—and expensive—scopes. The only exception to this is if you'll need to shoot at dusk (legal considerations permitting) or at night (which might be the case for those using a Mini-14 for self-defense).

Not all rifle scopes will give you the ability to pick out targets at night. Some are little better than the naked eye as darkness falls. But some will enable you to see nearly as well as expensive night-vision equipment would.

In order to provide a good view at night, lenses should be coated to allow light to penetrate them easily. Unfortunately, the literature that comes with most scopes does little to tell you how good the lens coatings are. Luckily there's a quick way to check this: simply stare at the front of the lens. Quality lenses don't act like mirrors when viewed head-on. Poor lenses will allow you to see your reflection clearly on the optical surface.

Once you've found a lens that has a good coating, you can determine how a rifle scope will perform at night by calculating its "twilight factor." You can figure this by taking the power of the scope (the first number given in the specifications) and multiplying it by the objective diameter of the lens (usually the number that follows the "x" in the specifications). The square root of the result is the scope's twilight factor. For example, the standard 4x32mm scope would have a twilight factor that's the square root of 128 (4 times 32), or 11.3.

Most scopes have twilight factors of 14 or less. These are useful only for daytime viewing. In general, higher twilight factor optics will cost you some extra cash. But when compared to the cost of night-vision equipment—running at thousands of dollars for a quality scope—as well as the need for special batteries and the fatigue caused by carrying it, quality optical scopes are a real bargain.

Occasionally you'll discover a scope with a twilight factor above 14 that's still poor for night viewing. That brings us to the other important factor you need to consider when searching for a scope: exit pupil diameter.

The exit pupil diameter is calculated by dividing the objective lens diameter in millimeters (the second number in the specs) by the magnification of the lens (the first number). The result is the exit pupil diameter in millimeters. (For example, the standard 4x32mm scope we used above would have an exit pupil size of 8mm.)

Unfortunately, there isn't much leeway in what will work well at night in terms of exit pupil sizes. If the exit pupil diameter is close to 7mm—or a bit less—the optical system will work efficiently in dim light. This is because 7mm is roughly the size of the pupil of the human eye when fully dilated in the dark. (As this demonstrates, the 8mm exit pupil size of the scope in our example will have even poorer nighttime abilities than its twilight factor suggests.)

Even scopes with high twilight factors may do poorly at night if their exit pupil diameter is larger than 7mm. In fact, scopes with a lower twilight factor *and* an exit pupil size of 7mm may outperform more expensive optics that have high twilight factors but not the 7mm exit pupil size.

What about scopes with exit pupil size of less than 7mm? These generally don't work well at night, either. This is because they have poor twilight factors. Therefore, the 7mm size is always best for use in the dark.

Assuming you've discovered one of the precious few scopes with a 7mm exit pupil diameter, it will be of use at night. Optics with twilight factors ranging from 16 to 20 are capable of providing superb views at night when only the moon is up to illuminate your target. A few of the more common variable scopes with a wide field of view will fall into the low end of this group, *provided* the power is set to give a 7mm exit pupil size (you should figure this magnification beforehand so you can dial it up when you need it).

Twilight factors over 20—which are, unfortunately, rarely found and quite expensive—can pick out targets with only starlight illuminating them. Provided the optics are coated properly, most of the scopes in this group will be in the 8x56mm range. Most are top-line European scopes with price tags in the $400 to $800 range; but this is still considerably cheaper than night vision scopes—and you won't even need batteries.

If you should be so fortunate as to find two scopes that have the high twilight factor *and* a 7mm exit pupil size—which is unlikely—then the one with the greater magnification will generally yield a better view at night. This is because the optics will cause more light to be concentrated into your eyes. On the flip side of things is the fact that higher magnifications make things harder to track due to a narrower field of view. Because of this, 8X to 10X will usually be the top range that you can use—and afford—in terms of power of magnification.

Small "combat" scopes have recently become popular among many daytime shooters. These give the shooter a small package that doesn't weigh much and isn't apt to get tangled up in the brush. But most also suffer from a narrow field of view and rather short eye relief when used on stocks with longer pulls—points potential buyers should keep in

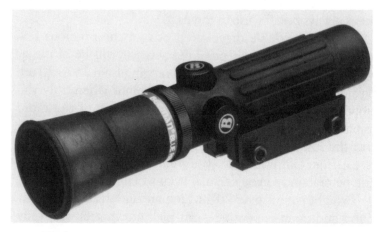

Beeman's SS-1 combat scope has rubberized armor to help protect it. Lightweight, it adds little to the load being carried. (Photo courtesy of Beeman.)

Beeman's SS-2 is a good example of the very compact scopes suitable for use on the Mini-14. The dial on the front of the scope allows it to be adjusted for parallax at various distances. (Photo courtesy of Beeman.)

mind. Among the best of these small combat scopes are the Beeman SS-1, SS-2, and SS-3 (with available-light illuminated reticle in the "L" models).

Another type of "small-package" sighting system is the dot scope, which creates a small red dot in the shooter's sight picture. Unlike other scopes, dot scopes generally offer no magnification, so they can be used with both eyes open. This makes them as fast as—or even faster than—iron sights and gives them none of the limitations in field of view that the combat scopes suffer from.

There are two basic types of dot scopes. One uses available light to create its (usually red) dot; the other uses a small battery to power an L.E.D. (light-emitting diode) that creates the dot in the scope.

The Armson O.E.G. (Occluded Eye Gunsight) is the best available-light dot scope and has a reputation for being the toughest one on the market. The shortcoming of available-light scopes is that they are only as bright as the light around you. Aiming an available-light scope in an area that's dimly lit and then switching to an area that's brightly lit can cause some problems. But normally, available-light systems work well, with the dot becoming brighter as the available light is greater.

At night, when available light is nonexistent, the Armson O.E.G. would be useless if it weren't for another light source: a tiny tritium element that gives off a dim, greenish-white light. This creates a dot inside the scope even in total darkness.

The Armson O.E.G. requires that the vision in both your eyes be perfect (or corrected), since one eye sees only the dot while the other sees what you're aiming at, so that the two pictures are combined by your brain into one apparent view of the target with the dot superimposed on it. People with sight in only one eye, as well as some who wear contacts or have eyes that don't track together, won't be able to use the O.E.G. because the dot will wander about or the two pictures won't be combined.

A version of the Armson O.E.G., complete with a mount to go on the standard or Ranch Rifle models of the Mini-14 and Mini-30, is available from L.L. Baston for $190.

The electric dot scopes aren't without a few shortcomings, but they can be used by almost anyone who can see out of at least one eye. And if you have both eyes open, they provide a wider view of the target area than any other scope.

Electric dot scopes range in price from $190 to as much as $430, so it often pays to shop around a bit. Since a small battery is needed to create the aiming dot, these scopes have to be turned on and off, and their batteries can run down. But provided you remember to turn them off after each use, it takes hundreds of hours of continuous use before it's necessary to change the batteries (which are available at most Radio Shack stores). If you'll be operating a dot scope in cold weather, it's wise to purchase lithium batteries. These will continue to function when most others conk out in intense cold.

Electric dot scopes can be used during the daytime or at night. Some, such as Aimpoint and Tasco, also have a 3-power attachment that permits them to be converted to long-range optical scopes. Most electric dot scopes (including the three major brands covered below) have polarizing filters to adapt to the brightness of the sight picture during the day. The brightness of the dots can be adjusted from a very dim point to a brilliant ball. Zeroing electric dot scopes (as well as the Armson O.E.G.) is as easy as zeroing an optical scope. One turret controls elevation and the other controls windage.

There are a number of electric dot scopes offered these days. Among the best are those offered by Aimpoint, Tasco, and Action Arms.

Aimpoint has been reworking and miniaturizing its

scopes so quickly that it's hard to keep up. Therefore, you'll likely discover some models not covered here in your gun store when you go shopping. All of the Aimpoint scopes are quite reliable, though the newer models are noticeably lighter and use less power so their batteries last longer.

At the time of this writing, Aimpoint offers three basic models. They're all available in black and, for the fashion-conscious, brushed stainless. The Aimpoint Series 1000 ($160) is designed to mount directly onto a Weaver base and doesn't require scope rings. The Series 2000 (which are being phased out) have 1-inch bodies that can be placed in 1-inch scope rings. The 2000 Long version ($230) is principally for rifles, though it will perform well enough on a pistol; the 2000 Short version ($210) is lighter and shorter, measuring 5.5 inches and weighing just 6.3 ounces. The current race among manufacturers is toward smaller, lighter scopes, and consequently, Aimpoint has added the 3000 Series to its lineup to replace the 2000 Series. The 3000 Series is nearly identical to the older 2000 Series but has a much smaller battery pack. The red dot produced by this new series is also smaller, making it ideal for long-range daytime shooting. The 3000 is available in a Short version for $249 and a Long version for $259. There are 3X scope attachments for the Series 1000 ($106) and the 3000 Long ($129).

Action Arms has marketed several different models of scopes in the past. Its newest and best entry is the Ultra-Dot, which retails for around $195. It has a 1-inch body, making it easy to mount it with standard scope rings and mounts. With the Ultra-Dot, Action Arms has reduced the size of its scope by placing the battery pack and control knob into small turrets (similar to those used to zero scopes). This creates a very compact unit that—at just 4 ounces—is the lightest currently available.

One nice feature of the Ultra-Dot is that its control knob

can be switched from "off" to "on" in either direction; this makes it easy to go to either the dimmest or brightest setting with just one click from the off position (unlike other electric dot scopes). The Ultra-Dot comes with several useful accessories, including extension tubes (to cut down on glare during daytime use) and a rubber eye shield.

The Pro-Point II series is Tasco's latest entry into the dot scope market. Unlike the Aimpoint and Action Arms scopes, these have 30mm tubes, giving them a slightly wider field of view than the 1-inch scopes. It also creates a slight problem in mounting them (fortunately, Tasco offers a mount for the Mini-14 for $44).

There are two versions of the Pro-Point. One is the PDP1L, which has its battery pack and control knob located in a separate tube attached to the body. The PDP2 has its control knob and battery mounted in turrets on the scope tube itself. The PDP1L sells for $350 and the PDP2 for $430.

The laser is another type of electronic aiming system that is becoming popular. Mounted on a Mini-14, the laser can be used as a sort of tracer. Unlike real tracers that zing out as the glowing tail of a bullet, the laser beam is relatively harmless, silent, and doesn't waste ammunition when used to locate the target. Once you have a laser mounted on a standard scope mount, you can flick its beam on and tell within a few inches where a bullet fired from your Mini-14 is going to strike from a distance of several hundred yards. And the rifle need not be shouldered. Firing from the hip or other positions can be quite accurate as long as you can hold the red dot produced by the laser on your target.

Some care must be exercised with laser sights since, in theory at least, the low-power beam they produce is intense enough to be potentially damaging to the shooter's eye. While you shouldn't be aiming a rifle at something you don't plan on shooting (in which case, the minor damage of the laser is not a concern), it's possible for the beam to bounce back from a target area and hit you in the eye when you accidently aim at mirrors, chrome, or anything else that reflects light.

Lasers are not the perfect aiming device, especially during outdoor combat when you're facing a group of opponents. In the darkness, a laser will be seen as a bright red light by anyone being aimed at. Lasers also create visible beams of light in fog or smoke and—as if that weren't enough—are readily seen with night-vision equipment. This is why these devices are rarely used by army personnel.

Another shortcoming of the laser is that it doesn't work well in bright sunlight, where the beam is lost. The laser is strictly a weapon for nighttime and indoor use when you're facing only a few opponents at the most, or for hunting at dusk when regular scopes can become useless.

In near total darkness, the laser is not ideal, despite what you might think at first. The reason for this is that in very dark areas all you can see is the small red dot—since the laser doesn't create enough ambient light to show what it is shining on. Therefore, you may still need to mount a flashlight (as outlined below) or have some system of illuminating your target if you're operating in very dark areas.

The price of laser sights continues to drop as they are produced in greater numbers and as less expensive lasers that can be adapted to laser sights are used increasingly in industry. It seems likely, therefore, that these devices will become competitive with electronic dot scopes in the near future. The main thing to remember is that laser scopes are very limited in terms of the number of jobs they can tackle. But if you do need one on your Mini-14 for dim-light shooting, then the laser sight definitely outshines other types of sights.

Aimpoint, Imatronic Lasersight, Laser Aim, Laser Devices, Lasersight, and Latron are among the best-known companies offering these devices, though other sources seem to be springing up all the time. Most lasers have shelf lives of ten years or more, and operational life is normally ten thousand or more hours if the laser is given proper care. Battery life varies from thirty minutes to several hours depending on the laser and whether it is flashed on and off or left on continuously.

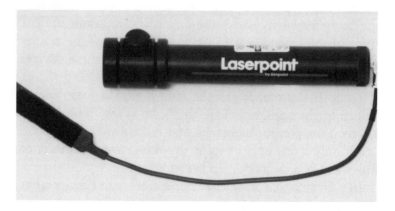

Among the best of the second-generation lasers is Aimpoint's Laserpoint. The unit mounts on standard Weaver-style rings and has a remote switch for easy control. (Photo courtesy of Aimpoint.)

Currently, the pick of laser sights are Aimpoint's Laserpoint and B-Square's BS-L1, which, being second-generation lasers, are compact, tougher than earlier laser sights, and able to run for longer periods of time (nine to sixteen hours) before a battery change is necessary (they use three AAA batteries). Both are relatively waterproof and are able to withstand a 2-meter drop—something many other lasers can't boast.

Like most other lasers, both the Laserpoint and the BS-L1 have elevation and windage screws for easy zeroing and a small switch on the end of a cord that can be activated easily with the thumb or fingers. When hunting or in combat, be sure the switch is *not* attached to the trigger—confusing the two could be disastrous. A better place to mount it is on the Mini-14's foregrip.

Lasers can also be used for cheap practice in areas where shots can't be fired. In this case, you would want the pressure pad over the trigger of your Mini-14. You can then squeeze the trigger/pad of an *empty* Mini-14 and see where the "shot" hits. With the batteries powering the laser lasting for up to several hours, each shot costs only a fraction of a cent as compared to twenty-five cents or more for .223 ammunition.

With just a few practice sessions, a laser can pay for itself as well as helping you become good at instinctive shooting (firing without using the Mini-14's sights). Best of all, you can practice in hallways or other areas where you couldn't normally shoot to get realistic "combat" training while honing your instinctive shooting skills.

Another aiming device suited for nighttime shooting is the flashlight. Not only does a flashlight mounted on the Mini-14 illuminate the target, it can also act as an aiming point at close ranges where the beam remains bright, since the flashlight is parallel to the barrel.

The primary shortcoming of the flashlight system is its limited range. Unlike a laser, which stretches out for hundreds of yards, a flashlight is reliable as an aiming system only within twenty or thirty feet at the most (though you can illuminate targets to a much greater range than that). A

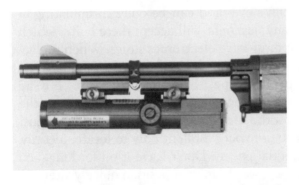

B-Square offers an under-barrel laser mount that is ideal for mounting either a laser or flashlight under the barrel of the Mini-14. (Photo courtesy of B-Square.)

flashlight also provides a dandy target to a foe if you're using it in combat. But if these tactical disadvantages are kept in mind, it's possible to use a flashlight mounted to the Mini-14 to your advantage, especially indoors or at night at close ranges.

B-Square manufactures a Mag Lite Saddle that is perfect for mounting a D-cell flashlight to their Under-Barrel Light Base, which fits on the underside of a Mini-14 barrel. The saddle has a curved base drilled to accept screws or bolts so do-it-yourselfers can also use it as the basis for a homemade flashlight mount on a rifle (perhaps by simply fastening the saddle to the lower handguard with screws). A flashlight can be fastened into the Mag Lite Saddle with the two metal strap clamps that come with it. The Mag Lite Saddle sells for $20, while the Under-Barrel Light Base is $30 for the blued version and $40 for a stainless model.

Of course, it's also possible to create a quick-and-dirty flashlight mount for the Mini-14. One way is to make metal brackets to screw into the underside of the forearm and use them to anchor hose clamps (available at hardware stores) that will hold the flashlight in place. Such an improvised system isn't nearly as precise as B-Square's, but it is considerably cheaper.

Flashlights with halogen or xenon bulbs can be used to dazzle your enemy's eyes and can be quite intimidating at night. Almost any flashlight will accept these bulbs, which are available at most large electronics stores. When replacing the bulb, be sure to match the batteries to it; many are made for a specific type of battery (alkaline, NiCad rechargeables, or carbon zinc). Matching the bulb to the battery can boost the life of both by as much as 20 percent.

Remember to use your flashlight only to locate, identify, or target a potential enemy. Don't leave it on for long, and be sure to scamper away from your position quickly after you turn it off. Otherwise, you're just asking for the bad guy to use your flashlight as his aiming point.

Since turning your light on and off quickly is an important tactic, your flashlight should have a momentary switch on it. Such a switch has the added plus of turning off if you drop your rifle or are downed by a shot; this will keep your enemy from quickly locating and killing you if you're wounded.

Remote switches on wires leading to the flashlight are a nice option since these allow you to mount the switch on the Mini-14's stock where your off hand rests. If you'll be using the flashlight mount in the brush, it's wise to secure the wires with tape so they don't get hung up on branches. Buy a quality remote switch and take good care of it so it doesn't become unreliable. Be sure to have spare light bulbs for the flashlight, as the Mini-14's recoil can be taxing on the light's filament and will shorten its life considerably.

Accessories Unlimited offers a black, rubber-coated flashlight with a detachable remote switch on a 6-inch wire for just $25. This assembly is easy to mount almost anywhere on the stock of a Mini-14 and is ideal for use with the B-Square saddle mount. The momentary switch on Accessories Unlimited's light can be epoxied in a handy location so the two-cell unit can be turned on or off easily.

Always test the flashlight you mount on your Mini-14 by actually firing the rifle. Some flashlights will go off during recoil, leaving you in the dark. It's better to discover this in practice than in combat.

Mag Lites enjoy a good reputation for durability, but they also have a high price tag. You may want to check out some other brands at your local electronics store.

Regardless of what type of scope or iron sights you decide on, the most important thing is to zero it accurately. The 25-yard zero is okay for quick-and-dirty shooting, but if you want precision, the 25-yard zero should be used only to get you into the ballpark for later ranging; errors of just a fraction of an inch at 25 yards translate into inches at several hundred yards.

For most of us, a 200-yard zero is best; then you can simply shoot point of aim with your Mini-14 anywhere within 300 yards, and all of your shots will fall within 9 inches over the entire range. A 200-yard zero makes it unnecessary to worry about bullet drop with most shots you'll ever make.

If you plan on making a lot of windage or elevation setting changes on your Mini-14, be sure to mark the "zero" spot with paint or fingernail polish. You might also want to study a ballistics table, jot down some changes for various ranges, and keep them with the rifle (maybe even tape them to the rifle's stock).

Whichever aiming system you choose, practice and you'll be able to hit almost anything you can see with your Mini-14.

CHAPTER 8

Of Robots and Remote Controls

T here's been interest in remote-control devices and robots for some time, with versions of both dating back to the beginning of the industrial revolution in Europe. World War I saw all types of rifles coupled with mirrors, extension stocks, and levers so shooters could snipe at enemies from the safety of trenches. And with World War II came remote-control machine guns on tanks and aircraft.

Today's technology makes it practical for do-it-yourselfers and inventors to create all kinds of remote-fire devices, from crude trip-wire booby traps (illegal in most areas of the U.S.) to computer-controlled robots with various types of sensors that will locate a target and train a firearm on it.

The do-it-yourselfer has a wide range of materials to aid in his creation of such controls for a Mini-14 or other firearm. Fiber optics, computers, and other sophisticated electronic devices are often as close as the nearest discount store or Radio Shack. With the techniques outlined previously in this book, you can join parts and tinker gadgets to create very complex control systems for the Mini-14.

With the caveat that most booby traps and "set guns" are illegal to create in the U.S. (because they are capable of injuring innocent bystanders), it's interesting to note that many types of booby traps are easily modified to pull the trigger of a Mini-14 rather than lift a noose to snare a victim. It's a simple matter requiring only a bit of thought to free a weight and thereby activate a gun's trigger.

Such booby traps can be activated with trip wires strung across paths or attached to doors or other objects. This will cause the Mini-14 to fire when a string or cord releases a weight connected to the trigger. (For a look at various types of booby traps that can be adapted to firing a Mini-14, see *Boobytraps: FM 5-31*, available from Paladin Press.)

The problem with such booby traps is that they are one-shot affairs and often easily detected. As such, they're not cost-effective for most people, and they also have the tendency to be unreliable under many conditions.

A step up in potential occurs when an electronic solenoid or similar device is used to activate the trigger of the Mini-14. Coupled to the proper sensor, this makes it possible for the rifle to fire several times, hitting any intruder the sensor detects.

In his book *Smart Bombs* (available from Paladin Press), Lawrence W. Myers outlines how to create such a system with off-the-shelf components. To activate the trigger, Myers suggests that by purchasing a 12-volt electric door lock actuator (available from Techné, stock #2504050) and adding a return spring to it, the do-it-yourselfer can build a device capable of pulling a trigger when a current is run through the actuator. The actuator is positioned on the stock of a Mini-14 with screws and homemade brackets. Adding a small rod gives the plunger of the actuator a "finger" with which to pull the trigger.

A wide range of sensors can be used to activate the electric door lock actuator. A trip to your local Radio Shack will yield burglar alarms that can relay a 12-volt jolt to set off the trigger. For multiple shots, it's necessary to modify these alarms so they're turned off by the actuator when it's cycled. This will cause the system to continue to fire if movement is detected or to discontinue if no motion (or heat, depending on the type of alarm) is present.

The infrared-beam systems used to activate automatic door openers or alarms can also be used to trigger the electric door lock actuator. Myers suggests that Radio Shack's Infrared Beam Security System (stock #49-307) is ideal for this when mounted on top of a rifle equipped with the actuator.

With this arrangement, the Infrared Beam Security System sends its beam outward toward a distant mirror (that is best hidden), where it's reflected back to the detector of the unit. Anyone or anything breaking the beam of infrared light sets off the alarm, which then triggers the actuator, firing a shot from the rifle (which should be lined up to fire parallel to the beam of light). This diabolical device fires once each time the beam is broken and—since it reacts almost instantly—will stand a good chance of shooting anyone walking in front of it.

Another device that Myers suggests using to fire a gun is the passive infrared sensor (which detects the heat of a human body and therefore suffers from few false alarms). Again, Radio Shack offers an inexpensive infrared sensor alarm suitable for such use (stock #61-2602).

About the only catch to such a device is that it has no ability to discriminate friend from foe—or even man from insect. And while a false alarm may be an inconvenience with a standard burglar alarm, a shot fired by accident is much, much worse. Such a device might have practical uses in warfare (they play a part in the movie *Alien*), but such an electronic booby trap is far from prudent for those interested those interested in deterring criminals.

A step up from such a system is a computer program that allows the "smart" booby trap to make some decisions as to the danger of an intruder and whether or not to fire upon him. Unfortunately, such sophistication is out of the range of the abilities and bank accounts of most do-it-yourselfers. But work is being done on such systems by businesses that market to military purchasers as well as by industrial complexes that house sensitive information and equipment. While the idea of a robot that roams about shooting at intruders sounds like a B-grade sci-fi movie, such devices are being created and, on occasion, fielded.

A better solution for most do-it-yourselfers is to put a human being into the command loop of a detection/rifle firing system. This makes it possible to let someone make the actual decision as to whether or not the remote firing device should be activated.

Again, the devices used for remote detection of an intruder and the remote firing of a Mini-14 can be as crude as a periscope and wire on pulleys (stretching from the trigger of the weapon to the concealed firing position of the shooter) to a battery-operated solenoid/fiber optical system used to see the target and cycle the trigger. One plus of the electronic system is that electronic pulsing of the solenoid would give the shooter the option of automatic fire from a semiauto gun with just one push of a button (though the legality of this is up in the air—a word to the wise).

With a Mini-14 that has a large-capacity magazine, solenoid control would also make it practical for the rifle to be mounted in a vehicle. A vehicle-mounted Mini-14 could be aimed in the traditional way, by lining up the vehicle with the target (as with most aircraft weapons).

A more complex aiming system would give a gunner control of the Mini-14's position independent of the vehicle's direction. Use of a motor-controlled mount could allow the gunner to move the Mini-14 along two planes using electronically-controlled motors. Very sophisticated systems using a joystick to aim and fire the Mini-14 might even be created by those with the time and resources to do so.

A more sophisticated setup for guarding fixed areas would consist of an alarm system coupled with a TV camera and Mini-14. The alarm would cover the area the TV camera tracked while unattended. When the alarm was set off, the human watchman/gunner would be alerted to check the camera, perhaps taking it out of its automatic tracking mode so he could search for the intruder.

If the guard found the intruder was dangerous, the Mini-14 (or other firearm) attached to the camera could be fired, using the camera to aim the rifle. The guard would be able to fire from a safe location with only the camera/gun mount exposed to the criminal's attack.

Such systems can be built from off-the-shelf components. Interestingly enough, TV cameras capable of "seeing" in nearly total darkness are available, making them remote-controlled night-vision scopes for all practical purposes. When creating a system that uses a TV to aim the rifle, it's wise to make the camera mount extra heavy and securely anchor the Mini-14 to the platform—but not to the camera, or the firearm's recoil could damage it. It's also wise to use rubber mounts on the TV camera in order to minimize vibrations.

Going beyond this, a camera/rifle combination could be mounted on a radio-controlled, motorized platform. This would make it possible to actually patrol large areas from a safe bunker, far away from intruders or enemies. While such a system would be vulnerable to radio jamming, it would be capable of dealing with common criminals who would not normally be equipped for engaging in electronic countermeasures.

Given the wide variety of devices available to hobbyist

and industrial purchasers, a vast range of remote-firing devices can be created around the Mini-14 rifle.

As you have seen throughout this book, the Mini-14 rifle is very inexpensive and durable. It's also adaptable to a wide range of uses and can be modified or adapted to suit a shooter's needs and tastes. Whether you're interested in creating a custom hunting rifle or a high-tech, remote-controlled robot, all that's needed is a little time and elbow grease to turn the rifle into a Mini-14 super system of your own design.

Manufacturers' Addresses

Accessories Unlimited
P.O. Box 1086
Stillwater, OK 74076
(Flashlight assembly with detachable momentary switch)

Accuracy Rifle Systems
P.O. Box 13772
Odessa, TX 79768
(Heavy-barrel custom modification of Mini-14s)

Action Arms
P.O. Box 9573
Philadelphia, PA 19124
(Ultra-Dot sighting system for Mini-14 and Mini-30)

Adventurer's Outpost
P.O. Box 70
Cottonwood, AZ 86326
(Accessories for the Mini-14)

Aimpoint, USA
203 Elden St., Suite 302
Herndon, VA 22070
(Red dot electric scopes and Laserpoint sight)

American Industries
405 East 19th St.
Bakersfield, CA 93305
(Calico M900 and M950 firearms)

Armson, Inc.
P.O. Box 2130
Farmington Hills, MI 48018
(Trijicon and O.E.G. scopes)

B.M.F. Activator
3705 Broadway
Houston, TX 77017
(Manufacturer of B.M.F. Activator)

Brigade Quartermasters
8025 Cobb International Blvd.
Kennesaw, GA 30144
(Military equipment and accessories)

Brookstone
127 Vose Farm Rd.
Peterborough, NH 03458
(Metal and woodworking tools)

Brownells, Inc.
Rt. 2, Box 1
Montezuma, IA 50171
(Gunsmithing tools and parts)

B-Square Company
Box 11281
Ft. Worth, TX 76110
(Scope mounts for Mini-14, gunsmithing supplies)

Cherokee
4127 Bay St., Suite 242
Fremont, CA 94538
(Manufacturer of Featherweight bipod)

Choate Machine & Tool
Box 218
Bald Knob, AR 72010
(Stocks, flash hiders, and
other accessories for the Mini-14)

E&L Manufacturing, Inc.
Star Rt. 1, Box 569
Schoolhouse Rd.
Cave Creek, AZ 85331
(Brass catchers, slip-on buttpad, and
other accessories for the Mini-14)

F.I.E. Corp.
4530 NW 135th St.
Opa-Locka, FL 33054
(Importer of LAW-12, SPAS-12, TZ-75,
and other firearms)

Fabian Bros.
1510 Morena Blvd., Suite G.
San Diego, CA 92110
(Mil/Brake flash hider for AR-15 and Mini-14)

Federal Cartridge Company
2700 Foshay Tower
Minneapolis, MN 55402
(Ammunition, including .223 "Blitz")

Firearms Systems and Design, Inc.
P.O. Box 19134
Minneapolis, MN 55419
("Ultimate" burst-fire device for Mini-14)

Gun Parts Corporation
West Hurley, NY 12491
(All types of surplus military and commercial
gun parts and accessories)

Harris Engineering, Inc.
Barlow, KY 42024
(Harris bipod)

Jonathan Arthur Ciener, Inc.
6850 Riverside Dr.
Titusville, FL 32780
(.22 LR adapter kit for Mini-14)

L.L. Baston Company
P.O. Box 1995
El Dorado, AR 71730
(Dealer of Mini-14 accessories and magazines)

Michaels of Oregon Company (Uncle Mike's)
P.O. Box 13010
Portland, OR 97213
(Rifle slings, recoil pads, carrying cases, etc.)

Olin/Winchester
120 Long Ridge Rd.
Stamford, CT 06904
(Pistol and rifle ammunition)

Omark Industries/CCI
P.O. Box 856
Lewiston, ID 83501
(Pistol ammunition)

Orpheus Industries, Inc.
P.O. Box 1415
Montrose, CO 81402
(Tri-Burst for 10/22, Mini-14)

Patton and Morgan Corp. (PMC)
4890 S. Alameda
Los Angeles, CA 90058
(Importer of ammunition)

Ram-Line
15611 W. 6th Ave.
Golden, CO 80401
(Accessories for the 10/22 and Mini-14)

Sarco, Inc.
323 Union St.
Stirling, NJ 07980
(Military surplus parts and accessories)

SGW/Olympic Arms
624 Old Pacific Hwy. SE
Olympia, WA 98503
(AR-15 parts)

Sturm, Ruger & Company, Inc.
Southport, CT 06490
(10/22, Mini-14, Mini-30, other rifles)

tAP ("The Accuracy People")
P.O. Box 24096
San Jose, CA 95154
(Adjustable trigger, "The Handle")

Tasco
3625 NW 82nd Ave., Suite 310
Miami, FL 33166
(Optical and dot scopes for
the Mini-14 and Mini-30)

Techné
916 Commercial St.
Palo Alto, CA 94303
(Electric door lock actuator capable of
being used in remote-firing devices)

Useful Publications

The following publications contain information that may be of interest to Mini-14 owners who are considering improving or modifying their firearms.

American Rifleman (monthly magazine)
National Rifle Association
1600 Rhode Island Ave., NW
Washington, DC 20036

Assault Pistols, Rifles and Submachine Guns
by Duncan Long
Paladin Press
P.O. Box 1307
Boulder, CO 80306

Automatics: Fast Firepower, Tactical Superiority
by Duncan Long
Paladin Press
P.O. Box 1307
Boulder, CO 80306

Combat Ammunition
by Duncan Long
Paladin Press
P.O. Box 1307
Boulder, CO 80306

Combat Handguns (monthly magazine)
1115 Broadway
New York, NY 10010

Combat Revolvers: The Best (and Worst) Modern Wheelguns
by Duncan Long
Paladin Press
P.O. Box 1307
Boulder, CO 80306

Firearms for Survival
by Duncan Long
Paladin Press
P.O. Box 1307
Boulder, CO 80306

The Great Rifle Controversy
by Edward Clinton Ezell
Stackpole Books
Cameron and Kelker Streets
P.O. Box 1831
Harrisburg, PA 17105

Gun Digest (yearly book)
DBI Books, Inc.
One Northfield Plaza
Northfield, IL 60093

Gunsmith Kinks Vol. I & II
Edited by Bob Brownell
Brownells, Inc.
Rt. 2, Box 1
Montezuma, IA 50171

Gunsmithing: Tricks of the Trade
by J.B. Wood
DBI Books, Inc.
One Northfield Plaza
Northfield, IL 60093

Home Gunsmithing Digest
by Robert A. Steindler
DBI Books, Inc.
One Northfield Plaza
Northfield, IL 60093

The Lewis Gun
by J. David Truby
Paladin Press
P.O. Box 1307
Boulder, CO 80306

The Machinist's Bedside Reader Volumes I and II
by Guy Lautard
Rt. 2, Box 1
Montezuma, IA 50171

The Mini-14: The Plinker, Hunter, Assault, and Everything Else Rifle
by Duncan Long
Paladin Press
P.O. Box 1307
Boulder, CO 80306

The NRA Gunsmithing Guide—Updated
National Rifle Association
1600 Rhode Island Ave., NW
Washington, DC 20036

The Sturm, Ruger 10/22 Rifle and .44 Magnum Carbine
by Duncan Long
Paladin Press
P.O. Box 1307
Boulder, CO 80306

APPENDIX C

Gunsmithing Schools

Barton Community College
Route 3
Great Bend, KS 67530

Colorado School of Trades
1575 Hoyt
Lakewood, CO 80215

Lassen Community College
P.O. Box 3000, Highway 139
Susanville, CA 96130

Modern Gun Repair School *
2538 N. 8th St.
Phoenix, AZ 85006

Murray State College
100 Faculty Dr.
Tishomingo, OK 73460

North American Correspondence Schools *
Oak & Pawnee Streets
Scranton, PA 18515

North American School of Firearms*
4400 Campus Dr., University Plaza
Newport Beach, CA 92660

Pennsylvania Gunsmith School
812 Ohio River Blvd., Avalon
Pittsburgh, PA 15202

Piedmont Technical College
P.O. Box 1197
Roxboro, NC 27573

Pine Technical Institute
1100 Fourth St.
Pine City, MN 55063

Professional Gunsmiths of America
13 Highway, Route 1, Box 224
Lexington, MO 64067

Shenandoah School of Gunsmithing
P.O. Box 300
Bentonville, VA 22610

Southeastern Community College (North Campus)
1015 Gear Ave., P.O. Box F
West Burlington, IA 52655

Trinidad State Junior College
600 Prospect
Trinidad, CO 81082

Yavapai College
1100 East Sheldon St.
Prescott, AZ 86301

*These schools offer correspondence classes in gunsmithing.